AUTHOR · **Leo Donato**

✉ leonziodonato@googlemail.com   ◉ leomusck

BOOK LAYOUT PROJECT · **Antonio Branca**

✉ antobranca17@icloud.com   ◉ igoxdesign

COVER · **Alessandro Romeo**

"MASTERPIECES EXPLAINED"

50 of the most celebrated art masterpieces of a times explained in just 60 seconds read each.

History, meaning, techniques, curiosities, anecdotes,
enigmas, mysteries and artistic stratagems
of the most famous artworks.

Leo Donato

This book is dedicated to Papa' Raffaele
and his goodness which were taken
away from us far too soon,
to the love, hard work and sacrifices of Mamma Maria,
to the beauty and sweetness of my sister Ida
and my niece Alice,
to Lina's smile and her always open door
which for me has been a safe shelter,
to the Star the shines in the sky,
to the continuous support of Teresa, Francesco and family,
to Alex, an unprecedented mix of patience, helpfulness, intelligence and
noble sentiments,
to the 3 wonderful "proof readers" and to their colleague,
to all my uncles, aunties, work colleagues and friends, hoping it will
make them proud of me,
to the United Kingdom, which taught me not to be afraid of change but
embrace it instead,
to Angioletto, my favorite rock star who, I am sure, from "up there", is
already having a laugh

INTRODUCTION

The book you are about to read comes directly from a personal selfish need, a personal "tool" designed to turn the awareness of my ignorance in desire of knowledge.
Over the last 15 years, thanks to hundreds of international work and pleasure trips, I had the fortune to visit the most important museums of the world and to admire the most celebrated art masterpieces of all time.
The sensation of privilege I felt in having the chance to see in person these masterpieces was, however, always combined with a feeling of inadequacy strictly linked to the lack of a solid cultural background which could help me understand their deepest meanings.
Beyond the subjective feelings which every artwork can spark in each individual's spirit, which are clearly personal, I felt the need, in order to fully appreciate them, to discover their hidden stories as well as the artists' "inner journeys" leading to their creation. My curiosity forced me to do the best to try to understand what makes an artwork a masterpiece and why a masterpiece can be worth millions of dollars.
Not being an art expert, I applied to this effort the research methods of the International Business and Technology Intelligence Advisor, job that I did over the last 15 years and which allowed me to visit more than 60 countries and to spend 12 years in the UK. Once again the "selfish" goal was to remedy my cultural deficiency, which otherwise would have remained there, unsolved, as a regret for the rest of my life.
The rest has been done by the Covid pandemic and the necessary limitations to our freedoms that it imposed, which, paradoxically, allowed me to devote time and energy to the attempt of summarizing and reassembling the results of my research within 50 reviews of single masterpieces, which could compose a book able to give the readers the chance to comprehend the "beauty" of each of them in just 60 seconds read.
I have tried, in other words, to solve the problem of the fragmentation of information affecting art, which requires whoever wants to approach the subject, to necessarily collect information from different, often partial and in different languages, sources (books, research papers, press articles, documentaries, youtube videos, events). This difficult journey acts as barrier to regular people willing to learn more, who very often do not know where to start or give up soon after trying as they wrongly assume the subject is too complicated and hardly accessible.
The initial selfishness, then, gradually made space for altruism intended as desire and need of sharing the results of my work to try to "help" whoever, like me, felt inadequate in front of the magnificence of art. The reader then, in the end, will be able to easily acquire knowledge about history, significance, techniques, curiosities, secrets, enigmas and artistic stratagems of the most famous masterpieces of all times.

With extreme respect of the "sacrality" of the subject, the book uses a simple and accessible language with the ambition of spreading the knowledge of art to the general public.
The book does not rank the artworks in terms of importance, being them ordered exclusively according to a chronological criteria taking into account the year in which the production of the artwork has been concluded, in a *"journey through the time of art"* starting from the Riace Bronzes (450 A.C.) and the most famous Greek sculptures, "passing through" the best masterpieces of Leonardo, Michelangelo, Caravaggio, Vermeer, Van Gogh and many others, and terminating with Picasso's Guernica (1937). Every painting description is associated with a picture which allows the reader to check in real time all the unveiled meanings, curiosities and mysteries. The final part is dedicated, with regards to each masterpiece, to the list of the consulted sources.

Happy reading.

Leo Donato

Contents

1. RIACE BRONZES	*12*
2. NIKE OF SAMOTHRACE	*14*
3. VENUS DE MILO	*16*
4. THE ARNOLFINI PORTRAIT	*18*
5. DEAD CHRIST	*20*
6. LA PRIMAVERA (The Spring)	*22*
7. THE BIRTH OF VENUS	*24*
8. THE LAST SUPPER	*26*
9. SALVATOR MUNDI	*28*
10. LA PIETÀ	*30*
11. DAVID	*32*
12. THE SCHOOL OF ATHENS	*34*
13. THE CREATION OF ADAM	*36*
14. LA DONNA VELATA (The woman with the veil)	*38*
15. THE GIOCONDA (or Monalisa)	*40*
16. LA VENERE DI URBINO	*42*
17. BASKET OF FRUIT	*44*
18. ECCE HOMO	*46*
19. APOLLO E DAFNE	*48*
20. THE CONSEQUENCES OF WAR	*50*
21. THE NIGHT WATCH	*52*
22. LAS MENINAS	*54*
23. THE GIRL WITH THE PEARL EARRING	*56*
24. THE LACEMAKER	*58*
25. THE SWING	*60*
26. PSYCHE REVIVED BY CUPID'S KISS	*62*

27. THE THIRD OF MAY 1808	64
28. THE GRANDE ODALISQUE	66
29. WANDERER ABOVE THE SEA FOG	68
30. LIBERT LEADING THE PEOPLE	70
31. THE GREAT WAVE OF KANAGAWA	72
32. THE NINTH WAVE	74
33. THE GLEANERS	76
34. LUNCHEON ON THE GRASS	78
35. WHISTLER'S MOTHER	80
36. BAL DU MOULIN DE LA GALETTE	82
37. A SUNDAY AFTERNOON ON THE ISLAND	84
OF LA GRANDE JATTE	84
38. CAFÈTERACE AT NIGHT	86
39. THE LADY OF SHALOTT	88
40. THE STARRY NIGHT	90
41. THE SCREAM	92
42. FLAMING JUNE	94
43. THE SLEEPING GYPSY	96
44. WHERE DO WE COME FROM?	98
WHAT ARE WE? WHERE ARE WE GOING?	
45. THE ARTIST'S GARDEN AT GIVERNY	100
46. LES DEMOISELLES D'AVIGNON	102
47. THE KISS	104
48. THE ENIGMA OF THE HOUR	106
49. THE PERSISTENCE OF MEMORY	108
50. GUERNICA	110
BIBLIOGRAPHICAL REFERENCES	113

1. RIACE BRONZES

(Unknown Artist)

The Riace Bronzes are two life size statues which depict two bearded and naked warriors dating back, according to the majority of experts, to the period around **450 BC**. Today the Bronzes are on permanent display at the **Archeological Museum** of **Reggio Calabria (Italy)**. According to the official version, they were discovered by chance on the seabed by Stefano Mariottini, a tourist who was diving 200 meters off the coast of Riace (Calabria, Italy) on the **16th** of **August 1972**. Some doubts, however, on the exact facts leading to the discovery still remain, reinforced by a 2019 investigation of the famous Italian TV Show *"Le Iene"* (The Hyenas) which seems to credit the discovery to some young kids swimming and diving around the coast of Riace. Researchers believe that the two statues ended up on the seabed in the I or II century AC, period in which Romans plundered many Greek cities bringing back to Italy hundreds of masterpieces. Other experts, instead, believe that the two warriors fell down a boat heading to Constantinople in the IV century AC.

With regards to the artists who gave life to the two statues, researches came up with different theories. Some think they are the work of ancient sculptors such as Phidias, Onatas, Myron or Polykleitos. More recent theories however attribute the authorship to Pythagoras of Rhegion, considered by Pliny the Elder the most skilled artist in controlling bronze fusions, the *"first one to reproduce nerves, veins and diligently the hair* (**Naturalis Historia XXXIV 59**).

Mystery also involves the identity of the two warriors which, for this reason, still today are referred as **Statue A and Statue B**. The Statue A depicts probably a *Hoplite* (citizen-soldiers of ancient Greek city-states) while the Statue B would depict a warrior King.

What is for now just a hypothesis expressed by some researchers, leads back the 2 characters to the famous play **"Seven against Thebes"** by **Aeschylus** in which seven warrior princes create an alliance to declare war to Thebes. Following this theory the bronze A would depict **Polynices** and the bronze B **Eteocles**, the two brothers born from an incestuous relationship between Oedipus and his mother, which were the 2 leaders of the warring factions. Much more certainty, instead, there is about the material the bronzes are made of, as well as, the artistic techniques used. The two statues were made of bronze using the lost **wax process**, a metal casting method in which a molten metal is poured into a mold that has been created by means of a wax model. Once the mold is made, the wax model is melted and drained away.

Despite the bronzes might seem at first glance indistinguishable in terms of style, the results of comparative analysis revealed substantial differences which, according to many experts, would results in dating them back to different periods and/or attributing them to different

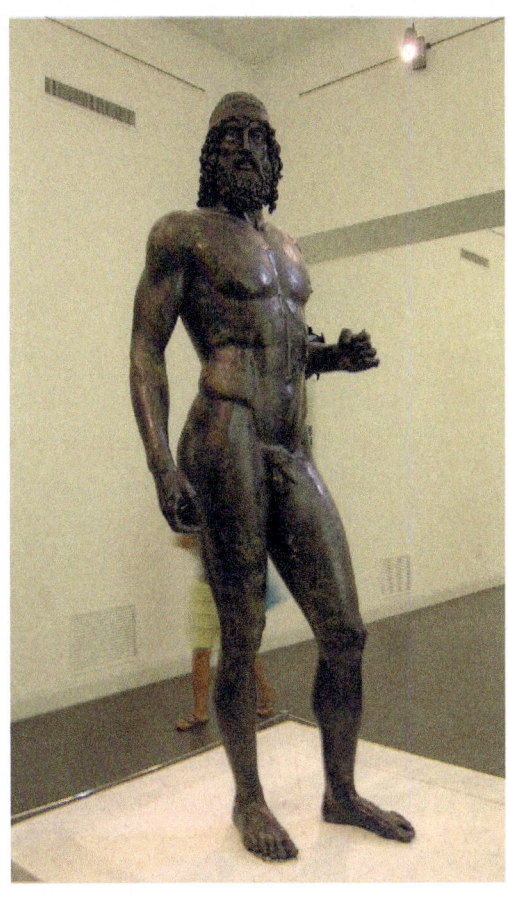 

Statue A   Statue B

artists.

The statue A, 198 cm tall, depicts the youngest of the warriors with his face slightly turned right. Many of the original elements such as the helmet, the shield and the spear went lost. Copper ornaments, still visible, were used to give shape to the mouth and to the nipples. Beard and hair are finely finished showing highly realistic curls which would have been created separately and welded one by one. The teeth are made of silver.

The Warrior B, 197 cm tall, also had a shield, helmet and spear which went lost. The feet are closer in statue B as well as the eyebrows are thicker and the beard little curls less finished. Statue B's hair looks like a unique mass whereas Statue A's hair appears as a set of individual locks and curls separated from each other.

Trapezius muscles are much more curved in Statue B compared to the square shape of the Statue A. Lastly, the body language e the pose of the sculptures show differences in mood and behavioral attitude

Photo Attribution A: Wikimedia Commons, Riace bronzes - Ancient Greek, by Luca Galli, licensed under CC BY 2.0. Photo attribution B: Wikimedia Commons, Bronzi di Riace - Museo nazionale della Magna Grecia di Reggio Calabria, by Effems, licensed under CC BY-SA 4.0.

2. NIKE OF SAMOTHRACE

(Pythokritos)

The "Nike of Samothrace", marble sculpture 5,57m tall attributed to **Pythokritos's hand**, can be dated back to around **200-180 BC**. Today the masterpiece is placed on display at the top of the *Daru* staircase at the **Louvre Museum in Paris**. According to the most likely hypothesis, the sculpture was created to celebrate a naval victory of Rhodes against Antiochus III, king of Syria, in the famous **Battle of the Eurymedon**, at the end of the III century BC. The Nike was discovered in 1863 without head and arms by the **French archeologist Charles Champoiseau**, who took it back to Paris where it was reassembled and restored.

The masterpiece is composed by a statue of Nike (the winged goddess of personified victory) in Parian marble and a base in Lartos (modern Lardos) marble which takes the shape of a ship bow leaning on a pedestal. The goddess is depicted standing in the exact moment she is about to "land" on the ship bow. Her weight is all held by the right leg while the left leg is just behind to seek the right balance. The torso is slightly rotated to the right while the bottom part of the body seems moving in the opposite direction, generating a little twist which attributes dynamicity to the figure. According to researchers, the left arm would have been lifted up in sign of greet and the right arm positioned down to hold a flag pole leaning on the right shoulder.

Nike wears a thin sleeveless tunic (*chiton*) made of fine fabric whose drapery, adhering per-

Photo Attribution: Wikimedia Commons, Nike di Samotracia, Musee du Louvre, public domain

fectly to the body, becomes almost transparent, revealing her sensual forms and creating the illusion that the tunic is wet as consequence of water splashes. The goddess appears also to be blown by a strong the wind which she faces with no fear. The chiton is partly covered by a cloak (*himation*) which falling from the left shoulder covers the hip and the right leg, leaving the left leg uncovered and reinforcing the illusion of dynamicity.

The best perspective to admire the statue is to look at it from its left side with a three-quarters view, a perspective which allows the viewer to glimpse most of the details as well as appreciate its incredible realism.

The statue is one of the most known examples of **Baroque-Hellenistic** (post-classic) Greek art, able to highlight action, movement and emotions. In its current version with no arms and face, Nike embodies the **value of the imperfection**, precious concept in a world that more and more chases models of absolute and unreachable perfection.

The myth of the Nike has inspired modern culture and artists such us, for example, **Carolyn Davidson**, a young student of Portland State University (USA) who, in 1971, designing what would have become the famous logo of the sports **apparel company *Nike***, took as source of inspiration one of the wings of the goddess of victory. Carolyn was commissioned the work by, at that time assistant professor, **Phil Knight** which soon after became the founder of Blue Ribbon Sports and Nike. The designer was paid 35 dollars (220 dollars in current value) to create what is with no doubt one of the most recognizable and iconic logos in history. However, in 1983, the company gave the well-deserved recognition to Carolyn, in the form of one million dollars' worth company shares as well as a diamond and a gold ring.

3. VENUS DE MILO

(Alexandros of Antioch)

The "Venus de Milo" is an ancient Greek sculpture dating back to around **130-100 BC** and attributed to **Alexandros of Antioch**. Made of Parian marble and depicting Venus (goddess of love and beauty), was found in pieces by a farmer who was digging near his land. The discovery took place in 1820 in **Milos**, an Aegean island. Soon after the sculpture was purchased by a French diplomat supported by the French navy stationing in the area, which unloaded it from a Turkish ship directed to Constantinople. Taken to France, the Venus was acquired by **King Luis XVIII** who, subsequently, donated it to the **Louvre Museum** where, still today, it is exhibited.

Many experts link back the loss of the arms of the statue to the fierce battle fought with the Turkish for its possession. Another theory, instead, opts for an assessment error during the assembling. In particular, researchers believe that the rests of what would have been the arms, were considered not belonging to the statue and destroyed as less finely finished compared to other parts. However, experts today agree that was common practice by Greek artists to spend less time on "less important" parts of the sculptures.

Subsequently new pieces were found in Greece, among which, a hand holding an apple, symbol of the island of Milos (Melos o Milos in Greek: apple in English) as well as reminder of the *"apple of discord"*, which Greek mythology refers to in the **"Judgment of Paris"**. In this case the sculpture radically changes, compared to the past, the narrative and expressive canons of the depicted story, showing Venus, thanks to a peaceful face expression, less erotic and warlike. This appears even more evident as a consequence of the reconstruction of the gestures of the goddess by the researchers, which would see Venus placing her left hand on a

---

Foto: Wikimedia Commons, Front views of the Venus de Milo, by Livioandronico2013, licensed under CC BY-SA 4.0.

support and holding an apple with the right hand, symbol of her victory in the judgment of Paris as to who was the most beautiful goddess between her, Athena and Era. .

The statue, 2.72 meters tall, is composed of 2 pieces of marble (upper part and lower part) joined under the covered hips of Venus. It is very likely that in its original version the marble was of the color of the human skin and that the goddess was wearing some jewelry. No trace is left of the color, whereas still today are visible some tiny holes which should be the hooks of the earrings, bracelets and necklace.

Although the style is certainly influenced by the early and late classic school, the sculpture clearly shows innovative contaminations typical of the **Hellenistic style** such as, for example, the contrast between the soft skin of the upper part and ruffled fabric covering the intimate parts, the spiral composition of the body orientation and pose which gives to the Venus a fascinating and sensual **"S" shape** as well as the undeniable erotic charge of the veil that seems to be slipping away and which in its original version was held by the right hand of the goddess.

The statue was originally displayed in a gymnasium, place traditionally conceived for the physical activities of young generations, which in Hellenistic times became more and more a place for multidisciplinary education. This particular collocation offers us a glimpse of how Greek cities told and passed on the stories of their past to the new generations. Furthermore, the presence of Venus in an education setting, could also be read beyond the erotic modern interpretations of her role, as the goddess protecting the young people entering the adulthood through marriage and sexuality.

"The Venus de Milo is an accidental surrealist masterpiece. Her lack of arms makes her strange and dreamlike. She is perfect but imperfect, beautiful but broken – the body as a ruin. That sense of enigmatic incompleteness has transformed an ancient work of art into a modern one." **(Jonathan Jones, The Guardian, 2015)**.

4. THE ARNOLFINI PORTRAIT

(Jan van Eyck)

"The Arnolfini Portrait" (1434), in an oil on wood (oak) painting of the Dutch artist **Jan van Eyck depicting, according to the majority of art historians, the Italian merchant Giovanni di Nicola Arnolfini e his wife Costanza-Trenta** in their home in Bruges (Belgium). It can be considered one of the most complex, rich of symbols and enigmatic painting of the entire Western history of art. In fact, still today, is not clear whether it was conceived to celebrate the couple's love and wedding or to commemorate Costanza who had died some years before. Although the first theory prevails in history of art books, there are some symbolic clues that, according to some historians, would go in the opposite directions: the chandelier is lighted only on Giovanni's side and one of the shoes in the background is placed outside the carpet.

Furthermore, a minority of researchers believes that the painting "immortalizes" a wedding ceremony including the payment of a dowry, a "picture" of the exact moment in which the couple is about to consume the first sexual intercourse, a necessary condition to pay what had been agreed. This old Italian tradition would see the groom holding the left hand of the bride in front of witnesses, as a sign of the imminent consummation of the marriage.

Despite the construction of the perspective leads to a perfect depth reproduction, recent 3D simulations showed that the painting does not have a comprehensive geometric consistency. It does not stick to the linear prospective rule of a single vanishing point, containing instead 12 vanishing points all spread around the central area. However, most of them have little im-

---

Foto attribution: Wikimedia Commons, Van Eyck - Arnolfini Portrait, Web site of National Gallery London, pubblic domain.

portance as they are related only to single objects. The first message that the painting conveys in undoubtedly related to the great wealth of the couple, expressed by many elements such as the chandelier, the painted glasses of the windows, the finely finished clothes, the carpet, the mirror, the dog and even the orange, whose possession in XV century Belgium is a clear sign of abundance. To the wealth showing function of the objects the artist associates also a religious symbolic meaning: the mirror is decorated with the 10 scenes of Christ's passion, the only lighted candle in the chandelier reminds of the presence of God, the dog symbolizes fidelity, the clog symbolizes hard work and sense of family, the cherry tree visible through the window represents love, while the red bed and the orange are old symbols of fecundity. The mirror reflects some people entering the room, widening the perspective of the viewer and making him part of the scene. The artist, in other words, manages to project the external world inside the painting. Above the mirror Van Eyck leaves his signature using the Latin sentence ***"Johannes de Eyck fuit hic 1434"*** (Johannes van Eyck was here in 1434).

Following the tradition of the other Flemish painters of that time, the artist depicts the light effects with absolute excellence and devotes great attention to the reproduction of details. For example, looking at the chandelier and at the window the viewer can fully appreciate the artist's ability in reproducing the light effects on different surfaces, which has made Van Eyck one of the greatest master in the oil on canvas technique. The masterpiece is housed in the National Gallery of London.

5. DEAD CHRIST

(Andrea Mantegna)

The "Dead Christ" (also known as the Lamentation over the Dead Christ or Lamentation of Christ) is a tempera on canvas painting (68cm X 61cm) by the Italian renaissance artist **Andrea Mantegna**, kept in the **Pinacoteca di Brera di Milan**. Some preparatory drawings kept at the British Museum date back the painting to around 1470-1474, even if the fact that it remained hidden for decades in the artist's studio does not give absolute certainty in this regard. Discovered by some members of Mantegna's family by chance after his death, the painting has certainly had a troubled life as from the city of Mantua ended up initially in Rome to then reach **King's Luis XIV court in France** and eventually taken back to Italy by the painter **Giuseppe Bossi** in 1807, who purchased it from the king's heirs.

Probably conceived initially to adorn Mantegna's own grave at the S. Andrea church in Mantua, the painting depicts Christ's body lying on a marble slab watched over by the **Vir-**

Photo attribution: Wikimedia Commons, Lamentation of Christ, pubblic domain.

gin, St. John and a third person (probably Mary Magdalene), who cry for His death. Mantegna masterfully uses the foreshortening technique in order to create the illusion of a perspective in which Christ's body extends in space. The artist manages, in this way, to eliminate any distance with the viewers, giving them the possibility to "enter" the painting, directly take part in scene and feel the pain of what is happening. All this represents a revolution compared to the traditional iconography of Christ's death, whose body had always been shown horizontally and in parallel to the viewer position, who had always been just a mere external spectator. Mantegna relies on "chiaroscuro" to obtain a perfect combination of light and shade able to give further expressive power and intensity to the depicted moment. Researches have proved the Christ's dimensions equal to a view from 25 meters from the viewer whereas, for the marble slab, this distance gets reduced to 2 meters. This artistic stratagem was necessary as showing Christ's body in that perspective at a 2 meters distance would have made the feet look too big, covering the entire view. To highlight the supine position of Christ, the painter places the light source above the horizon line, giving the viewers the impression that they are looking towards an angle. The scene is depicted with extreme realism with no space for idealism, using a "violent" style able to exalt the figures' details as well as their physical and emotional pain. In addition, the limited variation of colors of the painting, monopolized by shades of pink, grey and blue, reduces even more the space, increasing the sense of pain expressed by the painting.

The canvas is made of a fine twine of linen, depicting Christ's body from a perspective that goes from the feet to the head. The shapes and the wounds of the feet, caressed by the light, make the viewers experience the same vision that Mary Magdalene had when, in the past, washed those same feet with her tears: *'As she stood behind him at his feet weeping, she began to wet his feet with her tears. Then she wiped them with her hair, kissed them and poured perfume on them.* (**Luke 7, 38**). Christ's head, turned on His left, is peacefully resting on a pink pillow. John stares at him, Maria tries to wipe her tears and the third person with her mouth emits a groan that feels "audible" to the viewer. Mary and John's faces, for richness of details, look "masks" exhausted by the pain. The half-naked body of Christ, of which the viewer can glimpse the intimate parts under the sheet, emphasizes his human and mortal nature. The pale color of the body as well as the dangling head seem to deprive Christ of any sacrality, making him undistinguishable from any other human dead body. On the other side, the accessibility and vulnerability of Christ's figure can be interpreted as possibility for human beings to get close to Him, both physically and spiritually, allowing them to "await" with more serenity and confidence the resurrection. Christ's body, in fact, despite the crucifixion, appears almost sculptural with his intact musculature, strengthening the viewer' hope for the resurrection.

6. LA PRIMAVERA (The Spring)

(Sandro Botticelli)

"La Primavera" (The Spring), panel painting in tempera (203cm x 313 cm) by **Sandro Botticelli** dating back to around 1480, represents one of the most mysterious interpretative enigmas in the history of art as, the depiction of various mythological figures, is not traceable to one single literary source. Research gives us 4 potential interpretative keys of the painting: (1) the illustration through mythological characters of the facts leading to a marriage in Lorenzo De' Medici's (patron of Botticelli) family between Lorenzo di Pier Francesco de' Medici and Semiramide Appiani, (2) the death commemoration of Giuliano de' Medici and Simonetta Vespucci, (3) an allegoric representation of the spring coming or (4) a pictorial depiction of the neo-platonic concept of pure and spiritual love which takes form in the contemplation of God.

Without digging any further in the single interpretations which divided historians for centuries, what is certain is that, in all four of them, **chronologically subsequent events** are identifiable. In this respect, the painting is a story "told" from the right to the left of the viewer.

This unfolding of the story in episodes, absolute innovation in a painting of such an importance, seems to link back to the logic of some illustrative manuscripts of the Divine Comedy dating back to around 1450 and, in particular, the miniature of *"Il Paradiso Terreste di Dante"* placed inside the manuscript 36 of **Yates Thompson**, named after the English owner whose wife, after his death, donated it to the British Library.

La Primavera finds certainly inspiration from Poliziano's *"Stanze per la Giostra"* (**I, 68**), which describes a similar scene with the same characters. The first figure on the right with a bluish face is the god of the first spring wind **Zephyr**, caught trying to kidnap the nymph **Cloris**, fecundate her with his breath and, subsequently, as shown by the flowers coming out of her mouth, turn her into Floris, the goddess of flowers and spring. In the middle of the painting stands the goddess of beauty and love Venus. Cupid, her son, is above the goddess depicted shooting an arrow to the three Graces, symbols of chastity. The bodies of the three Graces are shown from three different angles of view which, together, show from different angles the different part of what is a single body.

The garden, in which over 500 species of plants and flowers have been counted, belongs to Venus, who raising her hand greets the visitors. This is clear also considering the presence of a myrtle tree, one of the many symbols of the goddess. The dark tone of the vegetation is mainly caused by the deteriorating of the color, effect balanced by the "shining" abundance of fruits and flowers.

Some researches consider the two spaces on the sides of Venus' head the display of the knowledge of the human anatomy by the artist, given the clear similarity with the shapes of the human lungs.

The richness of sources, references, details, meanings and interpretations make "La Primavera" a huge enigma that nobody has been able to totally solve. The solution then, probably lies with will of the artist to converge in one place historical, mythological and philosophical dimensions. The ultimate goal is, in fact, to stimulate different intellectual reactions which evolve thanks to a continuous negotiation between artist and viewer, allowing to the latter to find, every time, new meanings. The painting is today on display in the stanza (room) 10-14 on the II floor of the **Uffizi Museum in Florence**, the so called Botticelli room.

Photo attribution: Wikimedia Commons, Primavera-Botticelli, pubblic domain.

7. THE BIRTH OF VENUS
(Sandro Botticelli)

"The Birth of Venus" (La Nascita di Venere) is a 1484 tempera on canvas painting (172,5 cm × 278,5 cm) by the Italian artist **Sandro Botticelli**, commissioned by **Pierfrancesco de' Medici** (cousin of Lorenzo the Magnificent). One of the symbols of the Renaissance displayed at the Uffizi Museum in Florence, it does not depict the birth of Venus as the title might suggest, but rather her arrival on land (Cyprus) pushed by spring wind Zephyr after, as narrated by the classic mythology, she had been generated, already adult, from the sea foam. In fact, according to the mythology, Zephyr's wind was considered able to generate new life. The painting depicts **Zephyr hugging the nymph Cloris**, in a scene that symbolizes love. Standing as pearl on a shell, Venus is welcomed on land by a woman (the Horae of spring or one of the three Graces) who hands her a colored cloak.

The painting brings to life at least two elements of absolute novelty for the art of that time. First, the female nudity for the first time is represented trying to interact with the viewer through her gaze. Secondly, the subject of the mythological art, namely the artworks which are directly linked to classic sources. In this case, among the many description of Venus'

Photo attribution: Wikimedia Commons, Sandro Botticelli - La nascita di Venere - Google Art Project, pubblic domain.

birth, Botticelli find inspiration from Pliny, Poliziano and Homer: *"I will sing of stately Aphrodite, gold-crowned and beautiful, whose dominion is the walled cities of all sea-set Cyprus. There the moist breath of the western wind wafted her over the waves of the loud-moaning sea [5] in soft foam, and there the gold-filleted Hours welcomed her joyously"*. **(Homer, Hymn 6 to Aphrodite)**.

The goddess, ethereal and bright in her appearance, seems to put all the attention on herself, almost like she wants to contemplate her own beauty. This behavioral attitude, was, according to neo-platonic philosophy, the way to "elevate" the human souls to the divine soul. Among the different styles of depiction of Venus, Botticelli's one is surely a **Venere "pudica" (Prudish Venus)** of classical inspiration, with the right breast covered by her own hand and the intimate parts covered by her own hair. It is clear then the will of the artist to celebrate the real beauty, the one resulting from the union of matter (nature) and spirit (idea). The masterpiece recalls also the classical sculptures, in particular as a consequence of the use of the "contrapposto" style, which, leaves the balance of Venus to one single leaned leg. The artist twists the goddess proportions in favor of the research of harmony and beauty, addressing a higher ideal dimension. Venus's position, balanced in the most unstable part of the shell, is deprived of any possible realism. The same happens with the landscape, which, with the sea weaves appearing irregular and unreal, acquires a sort of metaphysic connotation, being illuminated by a soft and delicate light of which is impossible to identify the source, created with a gentle tempera technique.

Clearly then, once again with Botticelli, we are in the presence of an artwork which does not aim at representing reality but, instead, at triggering viewers' imagination, offering them different potential interpretative perspectives.

Beyond the depiction of Venus reaching the land, many see in the painting also the will of the artist to celebrate the De' Medici family. The arrival of Venus, in this case, would be a metaphor of the arrival in Florence of the kingdom of love, thanks to the cultural contribution of the family. This particular interpretation seems to be confirmed also by the presence of orange trees, called in the Italian of that time *"mala medica"*, a clear and not casual assonance with the name of the family.

Legend has it that to inspire Botticelli as a muse was **Simonetta Vespucci**, cousin of the more famous Amerigo, historically remembered for her extraordinary beauty.

The image of Botticelli's Venus has become, over the centuries, a real icon of beauty used in advertising of cosmetics and by other artists as a source of inspiration. For example, the king of the American pop art **Andy Warhol**, reproduced the face of the Venus coloring it in yellow, blue, green, purple and also creating a beautiful black version of the goddess.

8. THE LAST SUPPER

(Leonardo da Vinci)

"The Last Supper" is a mural painting by Leonardo Da Vinci completed in 1498 within the **Convento di Santa Maria delle Grazie in Milan**. The painting (4.6 m x 8.8 m) depicts the last supper of Christs and his apostles as narrated in the gospel by Mathew, John, Mark and Luke. In particular, the scene depicted reproduces the exact moment in which Christ announces to the apostles that one on them would have betrayed him, reconstructing all their individual emotional reactions through a complex mix of gestures, expressions and body language. The emphasis placed on the emotional reactions together with the ability of the artist to provide each character with an individual *"emotional dynamism"*, are the revolutionary elements which clearly distinguish Leonardo's representations of the last supper from the previous "static" representation of the same scene by other great artists such as Andrea del Castagno, Domenico Ghirlandaio e Pietro Perugino.

Jesus' figure is the central element of the painting, whose calm contrasts with the worried and incredulous reactions of the apostles who, turning to him, are able to direct the attention of the viewer towards the figure of Christ. The triangle created by the head and stretched arms gives solid stability to Christ's figure, further accentuated by the luminosity of the window in the background. From left to right of the viewer the apostles are: Bartholomew, James the Less, Andrew, Judas Iscariot, Peter, John, Thomas, James the Greater, Philip, Mathew, Judas Taddeo and Simon.

More than the picture of a precise moment, then, the Last Supper should be considered the "story" of the moments after the annunciation of Christ, which starts with all the apostles asking him *"is it maybe me, Lord?"* and ends with Christ reaching out to the wine and the bread, gesture which represents the institution of the Eucharist as described by Mathew (**2:26-29**): *While they were eating, Jesus took bread, and when he had given thanks, he broke it and gave it to his disciples, saying, "Take and eat; this is my body." Then he took a cup, and when he had given thanks, he gave it to them, saying, "Drink from it, all of you. This is my blood of the[a] covenant, which is poured out for many for the forgiveness of sins.*

At the same time Jesus and Judas Iscariot try to reach the same bowl, detail which once again is linked to the Mathew's gospel (**26,23-25**) *"The one who has dipped his hand into the bowl with me will betray me".*

Among the many reactions, Thomas, who points his finger up, seems to ask *"is this the divine plan?"*, with a gesture which anticipates the moment, after Jesus' resurrection, in which the apostle will use the same finger to touch Jesus' wounds and clear all his doubts.

Set in a humble and austere room, the scene is depicted using the linear perspective tech

nique, which resorts to parallel lines converging in a single vanishing point (right temple of Christ) in order to create an illusion of depth and direct the viewers' attention to the figure of Christ.

The windows show a green and heavenly landscape, reachable only through Christ.

The fact that still today we can admire this masterpiece is due to the great job of excellent restores, as Leonardo did not use the classical fresco mural painting technique which is carried out on a humid plaster or lime support helping the solidification of the colors. The artist opted, instead, for experimenting tempera and oil painting on dry plaster, a typical canvas painting technique which gives more time to the artist to correct imperfections but which, at the same time, turned out to be much less effective in terms of capacity of conservation. The state of conservation of the painting is today constantly controlled though a detailed monitoring of variables such as, for example, airflow, temperature and humidity.

The artwork, commissioned by the **Duke of Milan Ludovico Sforza Il Moro** is still today on the same wall where it was originally painted, inside the **Sanctuary of Santa Maria delle Grazie in Milan**.

Foto: Wikimedia Commons, Leonardo da Vinci - The Last Supper high. res., pubblic domain.

9. SALVATOR MUNDI

(Leonardo da Vinci)

The story of the Salvator Mundi is incredible: sold in an auction in New Orleans for 1175 dollars in 2005, after changing various owners, was acquired for 450 million of dollars (**the highest price ever paid for an artwork**) by the Department of Art and Culture of Abu Dhabi during an auction held by the famous auction house Christie's. Many think that behind the Department in realty there was the **Saudi Prince Mohammed bin Salman, who now would be the actual owner. Oil on canvas** (65,6 cm X 45,4 cm) dating back to around 1500, for which Christie's coined the name of *"male Mona Lisa"*, the painting depicts Jesus frontally and half bust, with the right hand lifted in a benediction gesture and the left hand holding a crystal ball, symbol of his universal power. Below his neck, set in his robe, He wears a small ruby symbolizing beauty and power. Moreover, at the cross of the two strips of His robe a pearl is visible, old symbol of femininity which probably Leonardo uses to represent Jesus' love for the entire humanity, male and female.

The painting raises to the headlines in 2011 when is displayed by the National Gallery of London and officially attributed to Leonardo, becoming the object of desire of museums and collectors from all over the world. In 2018, in view of an announced temporary exhibition at the Louvre, which was then cancelled days before taking place, the scientific lab of the French museum was given the chance to analyse the artwork. The conclusions of the work, illustrated in a book never published as a consequence of the cancelation of the exhibition, proves unequivocally the hand of Leonardo. With regards to the reason behind

---

Photo attribution: Wikimedia Commons, Reproduction of the painting after restoration by Dianne Dwyer Modestini, Getty Images, pubblic domain.

the last minute cancellation of the display there are essentially two hypothesis:(1) the fact that the museum considered the artwork not a job entirely carried out by Leonardo or (2) that the museum, despite recognizing the work as entirely Leonardo's, refused the condition posed by the owner of displaying the painting next to the Mona Lisa. According to the art historian **Matthew Landrus** (University of Oxford) in addition to Leonardo's hand, it is clear, as traditions of those times, the hand of one the painters of his studio, namely **Bernardino Luini**. **Martin Kemp**, other great expert of Leonardo, attributing the artwork to Italian master declared *"I wouldn't stick my neck out unless I was reasonably confident, but you can always be wrong. If I'm wrong, nobody died—somebody lost a lot of money ...'* A recent documentary with title **"The lost Leonardo"** pieces together all the facts leading to huge increase in the masterpiece price within such a short period of time, trying to shed light on the many mysteries that surround it.

Stereomicroscopic analysis have also revealed that the painting has been painted with a very limited palette of colors containing the lead white, vermilion, steel red, ultramarine blue, coal and bone black. A substrate of warm brown has also contributed to the creation of the whole atmosphere of the painting. All the elements, together with the addition pulverized glass, allowed the painting to reach the brightness, the translucency e the depth that we can admire today. Moreover, new studies seems to have resolved the mysteries of the reflex of the crystal ball and, in particular, the projection of the reflex inside itself, its anomalies and the three white dots. Through the use of *"physically based rendering"* technique as well as novel technologies, researchers managed to reproduce graphically the light and to simulate the reflex on the ball. The study confirmed the accuracy of the reflex painted by Leonardo, silencing once for all the opinions considering the reflex not realistic. Currently the painting is not officially kept in any museum, with media speculation placing it in a Swiss ultra-security art storage facility, awaiting that Mohammed bin Salman decides the right course of action.

10. LA PIETÀ

(Michelangelo)

The Pietà (Pity) is a sculpture by **Michelangelo Buonarroti** made of Carrara marble between 1498 and 1500, kept inside **St. Peter's Basilica** in **Vatican City**. Finished when the artist was just 25, the sculpture, sized 1,74m X 1,95m X 69 cm, is by far one of the most celebrated masterpieces of the Italian Renaissance. It depicts **the Virgin holding on her lap the dead body** of **Christ** after the crucifixion and before being buried. This scene, of which there is no trace in the Bible, emerges as event of Christian devotion during the Middle Age, when the clergy starts promoting a vision of Christ as suffering son and human being. Since then "the Pietà" becomes the subject of countless sculptures and paintings of which, Michelangelo's artwork, is certainly the highest point.

The sizes of **the two figures are not perfectly proportional compared to each other**. With the exception of the two heads, Mary's body is proportionally bigger the Christ's. This stratagem was considered necessary by the artist is order to make Mary look as she was easily sustaining Jesus' body. The difference in dimension is anyway made harmonic by the Virgin's drapery, whose folds clearly make her look bigger, allowing, at the same time, the artist to show off his technical excellence in shaping the smallest details on the marble.

Another controversial element is represented by **Mary's face, which looks too young** to be the mother of the 33 years old Christ. This depiction, which has been criticizes both at the time and in subsequent decades, finds justification in the will of Michelangelo to represent the virginity and eternal purity of Mary. Michelangelo himself, according to the biography written by his assistant **Ascanio Condivi**, referring to another of his sculputures *"La Madonna Della Febbre"*, said *"Do you not know that chaste women stay fresh much more than those who are not chaste? How much more in the case of the Virgin, who had never experienced the least lascivious desire that might change her body"*. Other historians link the youthfulness and solitude of Mary to the memory of the artist's mother Francesca Buonarotti.

A very important detail, difficult to notice, is that Jesus has one spare tooth, a fifth incisor. Renaissance artists used to attribute this additional tooth to negative characters as the *"tooth of sin"*. Michelangelo instead uses it to remind that Jesus, son of God, with His sacrifice takes on him all the sins of the world.

The Pietà is the **only artwork that Michelangelo has ever signed**. In this regard, **Vasari** narrates that the artist heard by accident some people looking at the sculpture, which, wrongly attributed the artwork to another artist. Being upset for what he had heard, Michelangelo decides to engrave his name on the statue, subsequently regretting this act of vanity and promising himself not to sign an artwork ever again. His signature, placed on the strip

leaning on Mary's chest, reads (in Latin) **Michel.A[N]Gelvs Bonarotvs Florent[Invs] Faciebat** "work of the Florentine Michelangelo Buonarroti".

The masterpiece, commissioned by the Cardinal Jean de Bilhères, ambassador of Charles VIII in Rome at the time of Pope Alexander VI, was initially intended to be placed at the Santa Petronilla church (where the cardinal had planned to be buried). Anyway, given the beauty and the great success of the artwork, it was decided to place it in St. Peter's Basilica in 1517.

Photo attribution: Wikimedia Commons, Stanislav Traykov and one more author - This file was derived from: Michelangelo's Pieta 5450.jpg (Cropped and cleaned version of Image: Michelangelo's Pieta 5450.jpg), licensed under CC BY 2.5.

11. DAVID

(Michelangelo)

The "David", sculpture among the most recognizable symbols of the Renaissance, took form from the hands of **Michelangelo Buonarroti** between 1501 and 1504. Made of Carrara marble and 5.17m tall, the statue depicts David, the hero of the Old Testament, as he prepares to face the Philistine giant **Goliath**. The Bible narrates that around 1000 BC, during the war between Philistines and Israelites, David, a young Israelite confident in God's help, manages to defeat in combat the giant, first by sling shooting him with stone in his head and then, after the fall on the ground of the giant, by cutting his head with a sword.

Despite the sculpture weights over 5000 kg, it was realized using a single piece of fragile and flawed marble, on which, 50 years earlier, Donatello had tried in vain to work on. Some friends from Florence written to Michelangelo, because *"was not out of purpose that of that marble, which was flawed, He, as had already done in the past, would obtain a figure"* **(Vasari, Lives of the Most Eminent Painters Sculptors and Architects, 1550);**

Differently from other artist such as Verrocchio and Donatello who had depicted David holding the head of Goliath in sign of victory, Michelangelo's version depicts the hero looking anxious with a ready gaze, in the moments preceding the duel. The tension of the moment seems clear looking at David's tightened forehead and neck as well as his swelling veins, all elements that the artist manages to channel in a body position that, on the whole, appears calm and tranquil.

The contrapposto technique, by which all the weight of the David seems to be sustained by

---

Photo attribution: Wikimedia Commons, by Livioandronico2013, licensed under CC BY-SA 4.0.

his right leg, expresses to the viewer a sense of movement and dynamicity. The head is turned left and the left hand is lifted over the shoulder to hold the sling.

Although Michelangelo was an expert of human anatomy, the perfection of the sculptured body hides also some small imperfections which become the stratagem the artist uses to highlights some parts. For example, in order to "bring out" the stone as symbol of courage and strength, David's right hand is bigger than the left one. The anatomic reproduction of the body is almost perfect, with the exception of a small muscle of the back, which the artist could not create as a consequence of a flaw in the marble, as Michelangelo itself writes in a letter. In particular, between the right scapula and the vertebral column, it is visible a small concavity, in a position where should have been sculptured the missing muscle instead.

Furthermore, according to a study by the **University of Stanford**, which, through complex graphic technologies allowed to see details otherwise not visible to the human sight, the position of David's eyes suggests that he was affected by *exotropia*, a form of strabismus which causes the pupils to move externally. In the case of the David, this condition affects the right eye which seems to be looking elsewhere in relation to the viewer, whereas the left eye steers directly at him. Michelangelo uses this deviation of the sight as an artistic tool to the benefit of the viewer, who getting close to the statue from the left notices that David's left eyes looks at him while, at the same time, the right eye steers astutely at Goliath.

The David is, with no doubt, one of the most famous sculpture in the history of art which celebrated over the years the spirit of Florence, a small city if compared to European capitals but which is able to win thanks to intelligence and astuteness. The masterpiece sounds also as a warning for the city's rulers to act with the same courage and determination shown by David. Initially placed outside Palazzo Vecchio, today the David is displayed at the **Galleria dell'Accademia** of Florence. To decide the collocation of the statue a specific commission was appointed. Among the members there were great artist such a Perugino, Botticelli and Leonardo. Leonardo's view for example, maybe hiding some sort of jealousy, was that the sculpture should have been placed somewhere out of the main way inside the Galleria Della Loggia, in order to *"avoid spoiling the ceremonies"* taking place in the Loggia. **Vasari's words sum up better than anything else David's beauty:** *"For in it may be seen most beautiful contours of legs, with attachments of limbs and slender outlines of flanks that are divine; nor has there ever been seen a pose so easy, or any grace to equal that in this work, or feet, hands and head so well in accord, one member with another, in harmony, design, and excellence of artistry. And, of a truth, whoever has seen this work need not trouble to see any other work executed in sculpture, either in our own or in other times, by no matter what craftsman".*

12. THE SCHOOL OF ATHENS

(Raphael)

"The School of Athens" is a Renaissance mural fresco, commissioned by Pope **Julius II** and painted by the Italian artist **Raphael** between 1509 and 1511. The masterpiece still today decorates the walls of the **Stanza (room) Della Signatura**, one of the four so called rooms of Raphael within the **Apostolic Palace in Vatican City**. When the artist arrived in Rome ordered the immediate removal of all artworks decorating the walls of the stanza, as in his idea each of them was meant to host frescos depicting one of four fundamental intellectual concepts: **Theology, Poetry, Philosophy and Law**. In this perspective, the school of Athens represents Philosophy and it is placed on the wall opposite another fresco called *"Disputa"* which, in turn, represents Theology, generating a clear symbolic contrast between religious and philosophic-scientific culture, between faith and reason.

The two main figures depicted, placed in correspondence of the vanishing point to attract the viewer attention, are **the old Plato and his young student Aristotle**.

Photo attribution: Wikimedia Commons, Raphael School of Athens, PDArt, public domain.

Plato's upward pointed finger links to his *theory of ideas* which considers ideas prevailing on the reality of the physical world. Perfection cannot exist in the physical world which is not as real, timeless, absolute, unchangeable as the ideas, which are *"the source of all things"*, residing in the transcendental and spatial dimension of the *hyperurarion* ("what is above the sky", in Greek). For Aristotle, instead, the real existence does not start and end with ideas, but in the "thought" considered as divine reason. That is why Aristotle is depicted with his arm reaching out towards the viewer, as a sing of his belief that knowledge e ideas are generated by experience, the so called **empiricism**.

Raphael with this painting manages to **"map" the entire Greek philosophical universe**, giving each of the philosophers depicted the possibility to "complete themselves" with the philosophers and philosophical theories which precede and/or follow them in a particular area of interest.

On the Plato's left, surrounded by his students, it clearly recognizable **Socrates** by his unmistakable gesture of using fingers when is chatting, as narrated by Vasari. On Plato's side, kneeling and writing, the great mathematician **Pythagoras** is depicted, a big believer in *metempsychosis* according to which, the immortal soul moves from a body to another. His face reminds Donato Bramante's one, the head architect at the service of the Pope Julius II. On Aristotle's side the viewer can glimpse **Euclid**, the founder of geometry, in the act of proving one of his theorems with a compass. Among the **58 characters depicted** is possible to recognize, form his back, the master of astronomy **Ptolemy** holding a globe in front of the other astronomer **Zoroaster**. Sat on the stairs there are **Diogenes** with the uncovered chest and Heraclitus who reflects before writing. The figure of **Heraclitus** was not present in the artwork's preparatory cartoon and, for his resemblance with Michelangelo, seems to be Raphael's last minute added tribute to the other Italian master.

The figure with long hair depicts, according to many experts, the classical concept of beauty whereas the statues depicted in the niches are **Apollo and Minerva** expressing that human desires and violence can be controlled only by the human reason. On the far right, next to the man dressed in white, a face looks directly towards the viewer whose resemblance to Raphael would "hide" a **self-portrait** that the artists uses to sign the masterpiece. The whole mix of characters, symbols, gestures and meaning make the artwork much more than a simple painting, a real and **"live story" of the evolution of the philosophical thinking**.

13. THE CREATION OF ADAM

(Michelangelo)

"The Creation of Adam" is a fresco painting by **Michelangelo**, part of his decoration of the Sistine Chapel carried out between 1508 and 1512 and commissioned by **Pope Julius II**. The famous decoration includes 46 fresco paintings with 343 figures depicted, representing one of the greatest masterpieces of the history of art. The magnificence of the artwork is summed up perfectly by the words of the famous German poet and writer **J.W. Goethe** *"until you have seen the Sistine Chapel, you can have no adequate conception of what man is capable of accomplishing"*. Within this overall beauty, the Creation of Adam, is the fresco which depicts, as expressed by the Old Testament, **the moment in which God generates the first man**.

The scene is represented with vibrant colors and great attention to details. On the right side, God floats in the air and, surrounded by a group of angels, reaches out with his hand towards Adam in order to transmit him the *spark of life*. The Creator is depicted with grey hair and beard, traditional symbols of wisdom and eternal presence. The pink color of His robe represents, according to the beliefs of the time, a combination of power and spirituality. On the left side Adam lies on his back with a hand on the ground and the other stretched forward. Despite his eyes are open, Adam's attitude looks passive, a clear sign that the gift of life does not come from the actual touch of God but from a spark transmitted by God without touching the first man. The dynamic energy of God lights up the painting and expresses in the

Photo attribution: Wikimedia Commons, Michelangelo Creation of Adam, Web gallery of Art, public domain.

"almost contact" the generation of life, becoming then the metaphor of how the divine and the earthly can never totally meet, of the abyss existing between God and man.

Adams' body, however, muscular and well defined in line with the classical art, shows strong similarity with God's one which is revealed by the robe, communicating what is the real meaning of the entire scene, namely that the man is created in the image and likeness of the Almighty. The two bodies are depicted mirroring each other to signal that *"God created man in his own image, in the image of God created he him" (Genesis, 1, 27)"*. In the creation act is God who gets close to Adam, to symbolize that life is a gift "granted" exclusively by his will. Under God's left arm appears the only female figure of the painting, whose identity still today is a mystery. According to some experts she should be Eva whereas, according to others, she would be Sophia, the personification of divine wisdom to whom the Bible reserved an important role in the creation *"The Lord brought me forth as the first of his works, before his deeds of old I was formed long ages ago, at the very beginning, when the world came to be" (Bible, proverbs 8.22-31)*. Sophia acts as custodian of the female appearance of things, as a go-between God the earthly world and as personification of Holy Spirit. The left hand of the Creator touches one of the angels, who, given the strong resemblance to the baby Jesus depicted by Michelangelo himself in another famous painting entitled **"Tondo Doni"**, could be seen as the attempt to reproduce the creation of Christ. In this perspective, the artwork has to be considered not just as masterpiece able to express Christian ideals and facts, but also, given its communicative power, as a masterpiece able to feed, boost and renew Christian faith, **reinforcing the primary role of art in the study and promotion of religion**. Some scientific researches focused on the similarity between the reddish form containing the images of God and of the angels and the sagittal section of the brain, which might want to represent the gift of intelligence of God to human beings or, in a more neo-platonic interpretation, that human ideas are part of a higher reality perception system which expresses itself through God. According to this theory, the artist would have used his great knowledge of human anatomy to express, using the brain as a symbol to express that human intelligence comes directly from the absolute power of God.

In order to be entirely perfect, innumerable times he made anatomical studies, dissecting men's bodies in order to see the principles of their construction and the concatenation of the bones, muscles, veins, and nerves, the various movements and all the postures of the human body; and not of men only, but also of animals, and particularly of horses, which last he much delighted to keep. **(Vasari, Part 11: Summary of Michelangelo's last years)**.

The Creation of Adam, 280cm x 570cm, is located on the highest part of the ceiling, on the central part of the vault of the **Sistine Chapel in Rome**

14. LA DONNA VELATA (The woman with the veil)

(Raphael)

"La Donna Velata" or simply "La Velata" (The Veiled), oil painting on canvas (82cm x 60,5cm) by **Raphael** completed between 1512-1513, depicts a woman wearing a sumptuous dress with gold finishing. The head and the shoulder of the woman are covered by a long veil, traditional symbol of the virgin which, at that time, was mainly worn by married women and which, in the case of the painting, seems to want to hide its deep meaning, inviting the viewer to personally find it out. A precious necklace made of amber pearls as well as a ruby and a sapphire jewel, old symbols of marriage, adorn her hair. The right hand leans between chest and heart showing religious reverence as well as a certain "closeness" to the painter. The right hand stretched towards the left part of the body contributes to create a horizontal dimension in the figure which, competing with the vertical dimension, establishes its majesty to the eyes of the viewers and separates it from them.

The historian **G. Vasari** describes the figure of the woman as *"completely alive"*, identifying her with **Margherita Luti**, the so called *"Fornarina"*, woman of humble origins and daughter of a roman baker (fornaio), which Raphael, despite his reputation of ladies' man, *"loved until death"*. The legend has it that Raphael was betrothed to **Maria Bibbiena**, niece of the powerful **Cardinal Bernardo Dovizi da Bibbiena**, but he married in secrecy Margherita, of whom he fell in love with after seeing her getting a bath in the Tiber river in

---

Photo attribution: Wikimedia Commons, Woman with a veil (La Donna Velata), public domain.

Rome. The marriage with Maria, which Raphael tried with all means to postpone because he was not really in love, was never celebrated given the premature death of the woman. Her tombstone located in Rome inside the Pantheon, next Raphael's one, reads *"to Maria Bibbiena spouse of him, which with death prevented the happy marriage and before it was takes away, still young lady"*. The belief the woman depicted is the *"fornarina"* seems to be confirmed also by her resemblance with the woman depicted by Raphael in another painting called **"La Fornarina"**, which depicts Margherita Luti bare-breasted. Moreover, the Woman with the Veil wears a jewel (pearl) set between veil and hair, which looks identical to the one worn by the "Fornarina". Some historians noted that the unstable positioning of the veil and of the right sleeve, which seem like they can fall at any moment, as well as the gesture of the right hand attempting to cover a dress that looks "unbuttoned", would confirm the theory of the existence of a strong intimacy between woman and artist. To make the mystery even more intriguing there is an astonishing resemblance of the woman's face with a self-portrait that Raphael painted years before. Eyes, lips, eyebrows and nose look totally identical, posing new and so far unanswered questions about the real meaning of the painting. Raphael uses the sfumato technique to produce what looks a mystical atmosphere created by the soft melting of light and shade, from which emerges also a three-dimensional perspective. In addition, through the details of the sleeve folds the artist shows off all his technical ability as well as his talent in creating artificially depth and space. The famous art historian **Ettore Camesasca** stated that in terms of definitions and precision of details, the painting could well have been called *"portrait of a sleeve"*. Although the face is oriented by three quarters left, La Velata's gaze and her hint of a smile reach directly the viewer, revealing once again desire and complicity. Surely then, Raphael's objective was not just to depict the reality he could see as good as possible, but also to transform and idealize it, making it perfect thanks to his artistic talent. The Woman with the Veil, whose attribution to Raphael's hand was not recognized before 1840, is exhibited today at the **Palatine Gallery of Pitti Palace in Florence**.

15. THE GIOCONDA (or Monalisa)

(Leonardo da Vinci)

The Gioconda (or Mona Lisa), oil on poplar wood painting (77cm X 53cm) on permanent display at the **Louvre Museum of Paris** is, undoubtedly, one of the most celebrated art masterpieces in history. Painted between1503 e il 1506 by Leonardo da Vinci, the Gioconda would depict **Lisa del Giocondo**, wife of the Italian merchant **Francesco** di **Bartolomeo del Giocondo.** Although this identification, based on Vasari's words *"Leonardo undertook to execute, for Francesco del Giocondo, the portrait of Mona Lisa his wife"* and on other important sources is the most likely, some doubts still remain. It is not clear, in fact, why a prestigious artist like Leonardo would have accepted a commission by ta simple merchant and, at the same time, there is no evidence of the actual handover of the masterpiece to Francesco. The painting, instead, stayed with Leonardo, who "jealously guarded" it until his death. Furthermore, the depicted woman does certainly not look 15 years old, age that Lisa would have been when Leonardo started working on the painting. In this regards, one of the most important experts of Leonardo, **Martin Kemp**, declared *"I cannot disprove this (Vasari's) identification – at least is not positively daft – any more than it can be confirmed"*. The woman could then be **Pacifica Brandani da Urbino, Giuliano de' Medici's lover** who died just after giving birth to their child. The painting in this case would be Giuliano' gift to their son so that he could remember her mother. As stated by **Antonio de Beatis**, secretary of the cardinal **Luigi D'Aragona**, who kept a record of a visit payed by the cardinal to Leonardo, in the selection that Leonardo offered for viewing there was: *"one* (painting) *of a certain Florentine woman, done from life, at the instance of the late Magnificent Giuliano de Medici…"* . This theory implies that there were two paintings of the Gioconda, one depicting Lisa and one,

---

Photo attribution: Wikimedia Commons, Mona Lisa, by Leonardo da Vinci, from C2RMF retouched, public domain.

kept in the Louvre, depicting Pacifica. Another theory, which hit the headlines in 2017 after the release of the documentary *"The secrets of Mona Lisa"* and based on scientific research proving the existence of various layers of paint in the wood panel, considers the painting as an **artistic evolution** which started from Leonardo's will to depict Lisa and evolved, thanks many touch-ups and adjustments carried out by the artist, in the "tool" through which he attempts to communicate to the viewer his vision of the meaning of life. The almost-mocking smile and attitude of the Mona Lisa reminds the viewers of precariousness of the human condition, inviting them, nevertheless, to live their lives with irony and at the best of their possibilities.

Mona Lisa's pose, directly addressing the viewer, represents a turning point compared to past, marking the start of **a new style in painting of portraits**. Mona Lisa stares directly at the painter and through him stares at all viewers regardless their position, distance and perspective angle. This is the so called **Mona Lisa effect** typical of photography, which takes place when the subject looks directly at the camera. Some recent studies, however, deny that this effect actually occurs in Mona Lisa's painting, bringing forward evidence that she looks slightly left instead. The use of the innovative technique of "sfumato" which melts light and shadow creating a mystical atmosphere, allows to reveal Leonardo's great knowledge of the musculature and the skeleton of the human face. The face expression, in fact, is characterized by a **slightly hinted smile, at the same time seducing and detached, representing Leonardo's idea of happiness**. The position of the hands, which the sfumato makes soft, communicates a feeling of peace and tranquility. The smooth ripple of the hair and the soft forms of the clothes show a strong sense of harmony with the landscape background, contributing in a crucial way to make the painting a masterpiece. The average distance, at the level of Mona Lisa's chest is rich of colors and elements (road, bridge) which unveil an inhabited environment. The wider distance, at the level of the eyes, evokes a wild and uninhabited landscape in which colors fade away creating the illusion of distance. From the "manipulation" of the colors then, which in the backgrounds fade away almost depicting the "thickness of the air", takes form the perspective. This stratagem is known as **aerial perspective**. According to many experts the landscape would be the "Valle Superiore dell'Arno", located in the countryside of Tuscany, depicting the Buriano bridge and the Balze del Valdarno, a series of sand and clays gullies. Other theories, instead, locate the landscape in Lombardy, at the river valleys of the pre-Alps. On the right side there would be the Adda River and on the left side the Resegone peaks. Although many in Italy still today claim national ownership of the masterpiece, it is legitimately in France. Leonardo himself in 1516, in fact, after moving to France, sold it for 4000 ducats to the King Francis I..

16. LA VENERE DI URBINO

(Tiziano)

"The Venus of Urbin" (1534) is an oil on canvas painting (119 cm x 165 cm) by **Titian**, the most representative artist of the Venetian Renaissance. It depicts a naked woman laying on a bed just before she gets ready for the **"toccamano"** (hand-touching) ceremony, a Venetian tradition in which the bride to be expresses her approval for the marriage by touching the hand of her future husband.

The painting, commissioned by **Duke of Urbin Guidobaldo II Della Rovere**, would depict his young wife **Giulia da Varano**, married when she was just 10 years old. According to this interpretation, the artwork was created when the girl was approaching her sexual maturity, with the aim of "teaching" her the loving attitude she should have had with the Duke. Although it had been a marriage of political convenience, through the painting Guidobaldo tries to persuade Giulia not to neglect the sexual aspects of the marriage, reminding her of the duties she had as a wife. The painting, helped by the great gossip around this relationship, reached immediately so much success that Titian and other Venetian paint-

Photo attribution: Wikimedia Commons, Tiziano - Venere di Urbino - Google Art Project, public domain.

ers were constantly asked to reproduce copies. Other theories worth mentioning, however, identify the woman with the goddess Venus, with a court lady or simply with an ideal beauty generated by Titian's fantasy.

Inspired by the "Sleeping Venus" of his master Giorgione, Titian manages to create a woman figure which, in terms of forms, erotic energy and expressive traits, will become the inspiration standard for generations of painters who will challenge themselves with the subject of the reclining nude woman. From a compositional point of view the scene is set in an elegant room of an aristocrat patrician house in Venice in the XVI century. The woman lays down on a red bed covered with white sheets and soft pillows, holding a relaxed pose. With one hand she covers her intimate parts and with the other one she holds some red rose petals, symbol of beauty and pleasure. The petals remind also of the ephemeral nature of the beauty which withers with time, without it having to make the love fade away. The woman steers directly at the viewer in an allusive and flirty way, with her forms highlighted even more by the contrast with the straight lines of the floor, bed, window and other elements of the room. **The woman's attitude, who instead of seeming embarrassed of her nudity stares at the viewer, represents the real innovative element of the masterpiece**. As she looks like she wants to establish a dialogue with the viewer, with the aim of generating erotic emotions, it was decided to hang the painting in the private rooms of the Duke. With the exception of some jewels the woman is wearing, her totally naked body illuminates a room which is depicted with dark colors. In order to make the figure more erotic the artist twists the body's proportions stretching further her bust to intensify her curves. A dog, symbol of faithfulness, keeps company to the woman, reminding the viewer that sensuality is allowed with the limit of being exclusively addressed to the husband.

On the right side of the painting background there are two maids, whose presence reveals the high social status of the woman. The maids seems to be trying to pull out from the cupboard the clothes that the woman will be wearing, is a glimpse of normality which makes the painting even more irreverent for the morals of that time. The kneeling maid, whose appearance reminds the one of a child, represents the wish of the artist to the couple for their future children. The Venus of Urbin is today on display at the **Uffizi Museum of Florence**, where it was moved in 1694 following the marriage of Vittoria, the last descendant of Guidobaldo II, with Ferdinando II de' Medici.

17. BASKET OF FRUIT

(Caravaggio)

"Basket of Fruit" is an oil on canvas "still life" painting (31cm X 47cm) completed between 1594 and 1598 by the Italian master **Michelangelo Merisi** known as **"Caravaggio"** and exhibited at the Pinacoteca Ambrosiana of Milan.

The basket, made of woven wicker, is placed on a flat wooden surface parallel to the viewer sight, in a perspective which does not allow to understand whether it is a table, a shelf or something else. The neutral and anonymous background makes the still life painted the only protagonist of the painting.

The masterpiece if rich of symbols linked to the **Classical and Christian culture**: the grape embodies Bacchus but also Christ *("I am the true vine, and my Father is the gardener",* ***John***

Foto attribution: Wikimedia Commons, Canestra di frutta (Caravaggio), user: Lafit86, public domain.

15, 1-8), the pear is a classical symbol of the woman and love, the fig is classical symbol of protection and salvation, the apple represents the sins, the peach embodies the trinity and its leaves, shaped as human tongue, are symbol of truth.

Through this painting Caravaggio, for the first time in Italy, establishes the principle according to which the depiction of still life should not have only decorative value but should, instead, become a pictorial subject with its own and independent artistic value. Caravaggio himself declared to *"put as much commitment in painting a basket of flowers as in painting human figures"*.

The painting allows the space, thanks to the mastery in reproducing light and shadow, to be defined by the shape, angles, solidity and composition of the objects depicted. Instead of idealizing the still life as professed by the classicism, Caravaggio paints its imperfections giving to every object personality and uniqueness. The master uses a "crude" and realistic approach depicting withered leaves, grapes gone bad and even a small hole caused by a worm in the apple, with the goal of showing the imperfections of the mankind and the inexorable passage of time. At a first glance the fruit, exalted by the white background, seems very colorful. If, however, the viewer focuses the attention on the single fruits' details, soon notices that the artists uses different shades of color. Light and dark, beauty and horror, pleasure and danger are constantly at play in nature and only maintaining the balance and continuously monitoring his moves it possible to slow down the unavoidable decay.

The viewers who look at the painting from their left side towards their right side can admire a vivid and bright depiction which, gradually, makes way for a darker representation in which the leaves become withered as a sign of the passage from life to death. Caravaggio in this painting, as in many others, paints the pure reality freed of any ideal interpretation, starting an actual revolution in the history of art, whose genius to be fully comprehended by historians will require centuries and will take place only at the beginning of 1900. At the start of the XX century, in fact, historic events produce a greater sensitivity towards the "true reality" devoid of any ideal element, rehabilitating Caravaggio as one the greatest artist ever who, in terms of contents, paradoxically becomes a contemporary artist.

Looking at the painting, the viewer, thanks to its extreme realism, almost manages to feel the nice smell of the grape just picked as well as the roughness of the leaves delicately placed on the basket.

The Basket of Fruit was commissioned by **Cardinal Francesco Maria del Monte**, one of the first to notice Caravaggio's talent. The Cardinal will then donate it to the Archbishop Borromeo who will declare *"I would have liked to hang the painting next to another one depicting a similar basket but none managed to reach a comparable excellence and beauty......so it was (hung) alone"*.

18. ECCE HOMO

(Caravaggio)

Six minutes, this is the time that **Massimo Pullini**, Professor at the Academy of Fine Arts of Bologna (Italy), needed to recognize, last March (2021), a painting of Caravaggio after he had received some photos via email by the Italian art collector Giancarlo Ciaroni, who had received them from an Italian art dealer.

After reading the email, Pulini replies *"Oh my God..... this is a Caravaggio!"* Ciaroni then informs immediately the art dealer of being interested in taking part in the auction scheduled for April in Madrid and managed by the auction house **Ansorena**, with a starting price of just 1.500 Euro. The news reaches soon the famous Italian art historian, writer, journalist and Member of Parliament **Vittorio Sgarbi** who, as reported by the newspaper *Corriere della Sera*, the 25th of March learns from Antonello di Pinto, artist e professor, that a painting apparently of **Mattia Preti** had been brought to the attention of an antique dealer. Pinto sends a photo to Sgarbi for an assessment who, as told by himself to the papers, says *"I see it, I understand the artwork is by Caravaggio and I think that, with the support of financier, I could bring it back to Italy"*.

Ciaroni however, for his part, tries to acquire the painting managing to meet up with the owners in Spain and making them an offer of 500 thousand Euro. The owners, three brothers, who had inherited the artwork for their father, explain to the Italian art collector that

---

Photo attribution: ANSORENA Casa de Subastas de Joyas y Arte en Madrid.

they had already received two offers of 3 million Euros each. Ciaroni then, realizing it was no longer a secret, provides the family with a report by Prof. Pulini which clearly identifies the painting as Caravaggio's Ecce Homo. The expression "Ecce Homo" (here is the man) was the expression used by **Pontius Pilate**, at the time governor of Judea, showing the scourged body of Christ to the crowd. At that time, Ciaroni tells, the amazement of the brothers becomes irrepressible… *"their father had purchased the painting in 1970 and, for 50 years, they had not even had the slightest suspect that it could have been a Caravaggio".*

In case Caravaggio's hand will officially be confirmed, the painting could obtain an evaluation of over 100 Million Euros. Since then, the artwork, titled ***"La coronation de Espinas"*** in the official auction's catalogue, becomes the center of an international case which leads the Spanish government to withdraw it from the auction and impose an export ban, awarding it the status inalienable national property.

The history of the painting dates back to 1605 when **Cardinal Massimo Massimi** holds a competition for the creation of an "Ecce Homo" in which Caravaggio takes part: *"I Michel Ang.lo Merisi da Caravaggio commit to paint to the Most Illustrious Massimo Massimi, after being paid, a painting of the same value and dimension to the one I already did of the crowing of Christ … 25th of June 1605"* **(Archive fam. Massimi, Rome)**.

Caravaggio did not win the competition and since then historians lose track of the painting, of which they will try to put together a timeline of all its movements which took it to Spain. It is the task of scientists now to establish the real paternity of the artwork, with many historians already confident it is a Caravaggio and others, as **Nicola Spinosa**, who initially considered the painting not a direct work of Caravaggio, attributing its paternity to the one of the master's pupils, the so called *"caravaggeschi"*.

More recently however (June 2021), after having the chance to assess the painting in person, Spinosa softened his position declaring that *"the painting is much more interesting than I initially thought seeing it on a photo. It is anyway necessary a restoration to have a definitive answer"*. Furthermore, a month later (July 2021), as anticipated by the Spanish newspaper *"El Pais"*, another of the leading experts of Caravaggio, **Maria Cristina Terzaghi**, drafted a scientific article that confirms the attribution to Caravaggio and, at the same time, tracks back all stages that took the painting to Spain. New developments of the story are expected!!!!

19. APOLLO E DAFNE

(Gian Lorenzo Bernini)

"Apollo and Daphne" is baroque life-size sculpture (2.43m tall) created by the Italian artist **Gian Lorenzo Bernini** between 1622 and 1625. Displayed at the **Galleria Borghese of Rome**, the masterpiece depicts the culmination of the story between Apollo and Daphne as narrated by **Ovid** in the *"Metamorphoses"*, a mythological narrative poem which involves Apollo (God of Poetry and Music) and the virgin Nymph Daphne, addressing, more in general, the subject of the frantic **search of a woman by a man who does not accept rejection**.

Ovid's story starts with Apollo's sarcastic comment towards **Cupid** (God of Love and Desire) and his abilities in using the bow *"What, wanton boy, are mighty arms to thee, great weapons suited to the needs of war? The bow is only for the use of those large deities of heaven whose strength may deal wounds, mortal, to the savage beasts of prey; and who courageous overcome their foes.* This comment causes Cupid's reaction *"O Phoebus, thou canst conquer all the world with thy strong bow and arrows, but with this small arrow I shall pierce thy vaunting breast!"*, who hits with a golden arrow Apollo making him fall in love with Daphne and, at the same time, hits Daphne with a lead arrow able to generate the Nymph's rejection towards Apollo. At that point Apollo starts desperately chasing Daphne who ignores the God's attentions and keeps running away reaching his father **Peneus**, God of the homonym river, asking for help. The God, on Daphne's request *"My dearest father let me live a virgin always, for remember Jove did grant it to Diana at her birth"*, turns her into a **laurel plant** to allow her to escape from Apollo. Also this new form taken by the Nymph, however, does not placate Apollo's

---

Photo attribution: Wikimedia Commons, Apollo and Daphne (Bernini), licensed under CC BY-SA 4.0.

love who tries to hug and kiss the plant, which, in turn, tries desperately to back out. Apollo decides anyway that Daphne would have become his plant *"since you cannot be my wife, you will at least be my tree. I will always have you, o laurel, on my hair, on my cithara and on my quiver"*.

Completed when Bernini was just 26 years old, the sculpture highlights the great ability of the artist to reproduce movement, transformation, sexual desire as well as fear and terror. **Bernini catches the exact moment when Daphne is about to turn into a laurel plant**: Apollo, covered just by a cloth tightened around the hips, grabs Daphne's torso, who attempting to escape leans forward with her mouth open as sign of fear of being caught and fear for the ongoing transformation of her body. Her feet become roots, her body is wrapped by the bark and the raised hands become leaves. Apollo's desire is represented also by his stretched left arm while the right arm tries to find balance, by his long hair touched by the wind, by his falling clothes and by the laurel twig reaching his groin. Moreover, Apollo rests on his right leg while the left one stays behind, with his slightly parted lips which seem sighing from desire and, at the same time, show all his astonishment for what is happening to the Nymph's body.

Bernini made use of **Giuliano Finelli's collaboration**, who finished some of the most delicate parts of the sculpture such as leaves and roots. Bernini's work was appreciated so much by **Pope Urban VIII** that He decided to create an inscription on the anterior side of the sculpture's pedestal in order to attribute to a mythological episode a religious meaning. The inscription reads *"Quisquis amans sequitur fugitivae gaudia formae fronde manus* implet *baccas seu carpit amaras"* (Who loving chases the joys of the fleeting beauty fills his hand of fronds and picks bitter berries).

Emblematic in describing the masterpiece are the words of Bernini's biographer **Filippo Baldinucci** which writes (1682) *"Immediately when it was seen to have been finished, there arose such a cry that all Rome concurred in seeing it as a miracle, and the young artist himself, when he walked through the city, drew after him the eyes of all the people, who gazed upon him and pointed him out to others as a prodigy"*

20. THE CONSEQUENCES OF WAR

(Pieter Paul Rubens)

"The Consequences of War" is an oil on canvas painting (206cm X 345cm) by the Flemish artist **Pieter Paul Rubens**, completed between 1637 and 1639. Artwork rich of symbols, it expresses the artist's condemnation of the tragic consequences of the **Thirty Years' war (1618-1648)**, namely a series of conflicts that involved European countries and caused over 8 million deaths. Fought mainly in central Europe, the war saw the participation of France, Spain, Sweden, Denmark, Netherlands, Poland, Austria, the Ottoman Empire and the Holy Roman Empire. Stared as a religious war between Catholics and Protestants, following the **decision of the Roman Emperor Ferdinand II** to **cancel the freedom of religion right** enshrined in the *Augsburg Treaty (1555)* and to impose to all citizens and governors to join Catholicism, it turned very soon in a war deciding who should have had the political, military, cultural and economic dominance in Europe, unavoidably marking its future.

Rubens describes the painting in a detailed letter sent to his colleague **Justus Sustermans**: *The principal figure is Mars, who has left open the temple of Janus (which in time of peace, according to Roman custom, remained closed) and rushes forth with shield and blood-stained sword, threatening the people with great disaster. He pays little heed to Venus, his mistress, who, accompanied by Amors and Cupids, strives with caresses and embraces to hold him. From the other side, Mars is dragged forward by the Fury Alekto,*

Photo attribution: Wikimedia Commons, Web Gallery of Art, public domain.

with a torch in her hand. Near by are monsters personifying Pestilence and Famine, those inseparable partners of War. On the ground, turning her back, lies a woman with a broken lute, representing Harmony, which is incompatible with the discord of War. There is also a mother with her child in her arms, indicating that fecundity, procreation and charity are thwarted by War, which corrupts and destroys everything. In addition, one sees an architect thrown on his back, with his instruments in his hand, to show that which in time of peace is constructed for the use and ornamentation of the City, is hurled to the ground by the force of arms and falls to ruin. I believe, if I remember rightly, that you will find on the ground, under the feet of Mars, a book and a drawing on paper, to imply that he treads underfoot all the arts and letters. There ought also to be a bundle of darts or arrows, with the band which held them together undone; these when bound form the symbol of Concord. Beside them is the caduceus and an olive branch, attribute of Peace; these are also cast aside. That grief-stricken woman clothed in black, with torn veil, robbed of all her jewels and other ornaments, is the unfortunate Europe who, for so many years now, has suffered plunder, outrage, and misery, which are so injurious to everyone, that it is unnecessary to go into detail. Europe's attribute is the globe, borne by a small angel or genius, and surmounted by the cross, to symbolize the Christian world. **(Letter translated by Kristin Lohse Belin, in Rubens, Phaidon, 1998)**.

In addition to condemnation of the War and all the tragedies linked to it, the artist offers to the viewer a way to avoid it. It is then the entire mankind that has to **choose between love (Venus) and violence (Alekto)**. The mankind is represented in the painting by Mars and by his gaze at Venus, a moment in which the God, as the entire humanity, can decide that love has to prevail on destruction.

The analysis of Rubens's correspondence, perfectly described in **Mark Lamster's book** *"Master of Shadows: The Secret Diplomatic Career of the Painter Peter Paul Rubens"*, alongside other historical sources, reveal, other than the great artist, the evidence of an **intense diplomatic activity carried out by Rubens to promote peace**. Taking advance of his accreditation in courts as a genius of painting, Rubens played a significant role as a mediator of the agreement between Spain and England which brought to the end of the hostilities. In another letter written after the peace treaty Rubens, as a further proof of his excellence in the art of diplomacy, anticipates the **Europeanist culture** which will be dominant after the II World War and which will bring to the creation of the **European Union**: *"I consider this peace an outcome that seems to be an element of union in the chain of Europe's confederations"*. Last but not least, in a time where political abilities were measured by the conquests of war, the painting fully discloses the pacifist ideals of Rubens which accompanied him in many other artworks. The masterpiece is on display at the **Palatine Gallery of Pitti palace in Florence**.

21. THE NIGHT WATCH

(Rembrandt)

The Night Watch is a 1642 painting by the Dutch artist **Rembrandt Harmenszoon van Rijn** on permanent display at the **Rijksmuseum Museum of Amsterdam**. Certainly Rembrandt's most celebrated masterpiece, the painting depicts, in a large canvas of 363cm × 437cm, an historical Amsterdam's civic militia (the so called **"Kloveniers"**). The painting was originally kept in the Amsterdam's Kloveniersdoelen, the headquarter of the civic militia. It was then, in 1715, moved to the City Hall. To adapt it to the new hosting wall, given the big dimensions, it was decided to cut some external parts in all four sides, which, since then, have not been found again. Subsequently the artwork was moved Rijksmuseum in 1885.

The painting's name, coined after Rembrandt's death for its dark background, is quite misleading. Many restorations over the years have, in fact, revealed that the background's darkness was mainly due to the dust accumulated over the years and that the depicted scene took place during the day in a place where natural light struggled to penetrate. The hand's

---

Photo attribution: Wikimedia Commons, https://www.rijksmuseum.nl/en/collection/SK-C-5, public domain.

shadow of the guard dressed in black on the uniform of the guard next to him shows clearly the presence of daylight.

The portrait of civic militias was a type of artwork very common in the Netherlands of that time, to which, Rembrandt gives a new personality, transforming it from simple depiction of lines of men into a live composition where every figure is carrying out tasks which define their role as soldiers. In the middle of the painting, dressed in black, stands the captain **Frans Banning Cocq** and next to him his lieutenant **Willem van Ruytenburgh**, dressed in white. The pair leads a military group made of 15 guards depicted just as they start moving following an order of the captain. Thanks to an amazing play of light the artist manages to create depth as well as a hierarchic order of the characters depicted. In fact, the faces of the guards with higher rank a clearly visible, whereas the ones of the lower rank guards are left out in the darkness. The guard dressed in red on the left of the captain, the guard behind his arm and the guard behind the left shoulder of the lieutenant carry out the operations of loading of the rifle, shouting and cleaning. Through the depiction of these three phases, the artist wants to highlight the ability of the Kloveniers in using firearms. The shooting man, of whom it is impossible to see the face, wears a helm with oak leaves, classical symbols of fame and victory. On the painting background, on the right side of the captain, between the soldier and the man wearing a hat and holding a flag pole, an eye appears from the darkness spying the scene. It should be the eye of the artist himself, who then decides to take part directly in the scene. About the identity of the mysterious girl wearing a golden dress there are different hypothesis which go from Rembrandt's dead wife to the personification of an angel. What seems more certain instead, is the role of *mascot* of the group played by girl within the painting. The chicken feet and the gunpowder flask tied to her dress are, in fact, traditional symbols of the militia.

The masterpiece has been victim of many acts of vandalism over the last century which, thanks to the most innovative restoration and reparation techniques, have luckily not left visible signs.

In 1911 a navy cook cut the canvas with a knife in protest for being unemployed, in 1975 another damage with a knife occurred by the hand of a school teacher who declared the he was carrying out a divine mission and, in 1990, an unemployed man sprayed sulfuric acid concentrate on the painting.

The Night Watch has also been at the center of conspiracy theories, like the one of the film director **Peter Greenaway**, who, in his movie **Night Watching** e subsequent documentary **"J'accuse"**, presents the theory, according to which, the painting wanted to denounce a conspiracy orchestrated against Rembrandt by the militia. This conspiracy would have led to the artist's financial ruin, who died in 1669, at the age of 63, alone and poor.

22. LAS MENINAS

(Diego Velàzquez)

Las Meninas" (The maids of honor) by the Spanish artist **Diego Velazquez**, example of baroque art painted in 1656, represents a genial **mix of realism and mystery**. Set at Madrid's Royal Alcazar Palace in the apartment in the past occupied by the Prince Don Baltasar Carlos who died prematurely in 1646, the painting is **much more than a simple portrait of the Spanish real family**. At the center of the painting there is the **infant Margherita**, the daughter of the King and Queen of Spain. Next to Margherita there are two maids of honor who had the task of assisting her: Donna Maria Augustina (left of the viewer), and Donna Isabel de Velasco. Among the other figures there are: the dwarf Mari-Bàrbola who had to entertain the infant during the breaks of the pose hours, on the right Nicolas Pertusato with his foot placed on the back of crouching dog. On the background the viewer can glimpse Marcela de Ulloa, head of the Queen's maids, in nun's clothes chatting with Diego Ruiz de Azcona, a court official. The man depicted painting is Velazquez who then presents himself in a self-portrait, whereas the figure in background, outside the door, is Marshal José Nieto Velasquez. The ceiling, which fills more than half of the painting, reminds of the structure of the landscape paintings, allowing the artist to effectively represent the space of which the characters are part of. The painting's main focal point is located on Margherita's left eye, through which passes an imaginary vertical

Photo Credit Wikimedia Commons, *The Prado in Google Earth: Home - 7th level of zoom*, public domain.

straight line dividing the painting in two equal parts. In describing the complex geometric structure of the painting, the famous Hungarian art historian **Charles de Tolnay** stated: *"the frames of the paintings on the wall...and of the door in the background compose a system of verticals and horizontal lines which determines the placing of the heads of the figures – so that what at first appears as an arbitrary disposition is in truth fixed to a well-thought-out but hidden plan. There is a threefold of gradation in the substantiality of the figures according to the distance from the beholder: those in the first plane are the most plastic – they form a triangle in the lower right corner, a kind of frame and repoussoir at the same time... those in the second plane are more pictorial; those in the third plane are shadow-like".*

Hands and faces are characterized by a certain degree of blur as a consequences of the use of (very) wet pigments, effect visible also on the upper part of the room and on the farthest background and which contributes to the creation of hazy and tangible atmosphere that made the painting so iconic. People features and forms become clearer as the viewer moves towards the deepest part of the painting, until reaching the maximum clarity in the mirror image reflection, created with a few quick brushstrokes.

The element that makes "Las Meninas" a masterpiece is certainly represented by its **unique perspective**. The artist, infant and Mari-Bàrbola's gazes are addressed to the viewers, who seems to become themselves the subjects to be painted. Rationally the viewers know that they cannot be part of a 1656 painting, but, given the self-reflected portrait of the artist, the painting almost becomes an optical illusion which **confuses the viewers, taking away from them any certainty about where they are in relation to it**. Widening the view it is possible to glimpse a frame depicting the King of Spain Philip IV and the Queen Mariana, detail that poses further questions. **Is it a painting or a mirror (as many think)? If it is a mirror, the subject of the painting could then be the couple rather than the viewer?**

A different interpretation is that the King and the Queen were visiting the artist's studio while Margherita and the artist stop to welcome them. Of this and other mysteries of the painting probably there will never be a unique answer, but what is certain instead is that the artist managed to capture a real and precise moment long before photography was invented. But is the **Velazquez's will to confuse the viewer** which gives to the painting a huge communicative power going far beyond the characters depicted. The masterpiece, an oil on canvas 3.18m X 2.76m, is on display at **the National Museum of Prado in Madrid**.

23. THE GIRL WITH THE PEARL EARRING

(Jan Vermeer)

"The Girl with the Pearl Earring", oil on canvas (44,5cm ×39cm) painted by the Dutch artist **Jan Vermeer** between 1665 and 1666, is today kept on display at **The Mauritshuis Museum in The Hague (Netherlands)**. The masterpiece belongs to the category of the *"Tronie"* (meaning "face" in XVII century Dutch), typical portraits by Dutch artists which, differently from traditional portraits, depicted regular people with "peculiar" face expressions often wearing sumptuous dresses.

Considered the *North's Mona Lisa*, the artwork depicts, standing out from a dark background, a girl turned left wearing a gold jacket, a turban and a big pearl earring. With regards to the identity of the girl there are different hypothesis which identify her with (1) one of the artist's daughters, (2) a maid or (3) just a product of Vermeer's fantasy meant to express his vision of reality.

Although Vermeer's characters are usually placed in "intimate" atmospheres associated to a certain "distance" from the viewer, almost as they were part of a theatrical scene to which one can witness but not directly take part, in the Girl's case, the gaze is directly pointed towards the viewer who feels invited to join her.

The points of light, located on the girl's eyes, mouth and pearl, are created through single and intense white brushstrokes which produce a glittering effect able to attract the viewer who does not even realize that the girl does not have eyebrows (did you realize that?), as the artist wants to communicate that in front of so much beauty details don't count.

The half-closed (or half-opened) lips show with incredible realism small signs of saliva as the girl has just said something that the viewer will never be able to know, deepening the mystery and **turning the girl from pictorial subject into a psychological** one whose real

---

Wikimedia Commons, source: https://www.mauritshuis.nl/, by Agatyr, public domain.

mood remains enigmatic and indecipherable. Still today the viewer wonders...*who is the girl? Why was she painted? What is she thinking of? Why is she wearing clothes which are not typical of Dutch girls? What does the pearl represent? Is her smile seductive or innocent?*

The answers perhaps need to be sought within the changing social and political context of the Netherlands' XVII century, which finally freed by the Spanish domination, was seeing the rise of a new merchant class "untied" from the traditional cultural and religious references, launching a new and modern political, economic and social perspective.

The turban then could be seen as symbol of internationality of the merchant class as well as the pearl could be considered as a symbol of its wealth.

The canvas is composed by different layers, a technique which allowed the artist to create a three-dimensional space, light plays and give color to the different parts of the painting.

The words used by British writer **E. V. Lucas in his book "Vermeer of Delft" (1922)** to describe the masterpiece *"Holland's most beautiful thing"* and the girls' lips *"a miracle as a Darwin tulip"* still today ring out.

In 1999, inspired by the painting, **Tracy Chevalier wrote the novel "The Girl with the pearl earring"** in which imagines that the girl was a 16 years old maid working at the artist's house.

The novel was then followed, in 2003, by a movie with the same title featuring **Scarlett Johansson and directed by Peter Webber**.

All this contributed to make the painting even more famous in recent times, "granting" to the girl the status **modern icon of beauty and mystery.**

24. THE LACEMAKER

(Jan Vermeer)

"The Lacemaker", oil on canvas painting by Jan Vermeer dating back to around 1669-1671, is on permanent display at the **Louvre Museum in Paris**. It is certainly one of the most famous paintings in the world, so beautiful that the painter **Renoir** defined it as *"the most beautiful painting in the world"*. It depicts a yellow dressed woman focused on sewing a dress as **symbol of the greatness of the domestic virtues**. The depiction of scenes of women carrying out domestic duties was a frequent subject in the Dutch art of that time, used to exalt some cultural values considered fundamental such as family, private dimension, industriousness and comfort. Despite the painting's small dimensions (24.5 cm × 21 cm), the artist manages to create a perspective made of various levels of definition able to address the viewer's attention towards the woman and the activity she is carrying out. This effect is further emphasized by the scarcity of the face's details which, alongside the orientation of woman's eyes look, make the sewing the central element of the painting.

The meticulous task of the Lacemaker is depicted in detail as shown by the realism of the thin white thread stretching through her fingers.

The more the viewer gets away from the woman, however, the more the forms become blurry including, paradoxically, also the close-up ones.

The white and red threads hanging from the pillow, for example, almost look some sort abstract dribbles of color.

The woman is totally absorbed by her work, unaware of the presence of the viewer and part of an ideal dimension showing us what things should look like rather than how they actually

Photo attribution: Wikimedia Commons, Musée du Louvre, by Jan Arkesteijn public domain.

appear. The painting also unveils **Vermeer's genius in using light** which, coming mainly from the right side, allows colors to "melt-up" in a lively play of shadows which do not leave any surface in one single color.

The slices of light illuminating the woman's forehead and fingers highlight the high precision and vision clarity needed to carry out the lacemaking.

The space occupied by the face and by the hands of the woman is surrounded by curve forms (curls, tied hair, sleeves and shoulders) which in no way interfere or compete with the centrality of her figure.

Even the fact that she is depicted with an anonymous white wall as a background underlines the will of the artist to avoid any details which could potentially distract the viewer from looking at the woman and at the activity she is carrying out.

Despite the closeness of the Lacemaker, the viewer seems not to be able to ever reach her, separated by a pillow, a small table and by the mystery of her work "hidden" behind her right hand.

This is a typical trait of Vermeer's art, known as *"poetry of silence"*, which aims at placing the protagonists of his paintings in a world separated from the viewer's one.

The small book, probably the Bible, gives a sacred dimensions to the painting which, once again, never interferes with the central figure.

According to many art historians, Vermeer would have used the **camera obscura** to reconstruct and represent visual aspects which normally would not have been visible to the human eye.

The tool was equipped with lens, mirrors and a sort of box through which the images were projected on a screen, allowing to see the smallest details and to create the photo-like effect that characterizes the artwork. Vermeer's attention, however, is always focused on the woman, on the "art" of sewing and, more in general, on the **creative skills of the human being**.

25. THE SWING

(Jean-Honoré Fragonard)

"The Swing", also known as "The Happy Accidents of the Swing", is a 1767 oil on canvas painting by the French artist **Jean-Honoré Fragonard**. One of the London's **Wallace Collection best pieces**, it is considered among the masterpieces of the **Rococo era** (post-baroque), which introduces in art more lightness, frivolity, delicateness and sense of provocation. Born as elegant and lavish decorative style, painting translates it into a pictorial style made of soft colors, blurred outlines, playful lines, curved shapes and more audacious scenes.

The painting resumes an artist topic, the swing and the pleasant dizziness as a consequence of its oscillation, which was traditionally used to symbolize leisure and love activities of the aristocratic classes. Fragonard, linking the swing to a female image goes beyond this meaning, engaging in a dialogue with the viewers able to feed their imagination within a scene rich of symbols which tells a real erotic story. In the middle of the painting, a young woman wearing a pink dress maliciously throwing one of her high-heeled shoes towards a sculpture and gazing, at the same time, at the man hiding in the bushes. The shoe represents the woman indulging in her passions while the bare foot symbolizes the lost virginity. The fact that the woman intentionally lifts her left leg, making visible her calf covered by white leg socks as well as a pink garter, represent another clear erotic message of the painting. This winking attitude marks the **woman's rejection of the social conventions** of that time, which limited

Photo attribution: Wikimedia Commons, The Wallance Collection, by Kaendler1710, public domain.

women in expressing their love and erotic desires and which are represented in the painting by swing's ropes.

The man hiding in the bushes peeks under the woman's dress, whose layers open up as rose petals, with a wicked smile. The hat, which in Rococo was used as a mean to hide an "erection", in the painting is removed as a sign of excitement and passion. Furthermore, the fact that the hat is touching the sprouting flowers, seems to symbolize an actual sexual intercourse. On the left side of the woman is visible the figure of an old smiling man, probably the woman's husband, who pulls the swing's reins totally unaware of what is happening around him. The shoe is thrown towards a statue depicting **Cupid** (God of Desire) resembling the sculpture *"Glamour Menaçant"* (menacing love) by **Etienne-Maurice Falconet**, which is considered a timeless symbol of eroticism. Although the characters are not identifiable with real people, their style as well as the fact they are depicted in recreational activities clearly suggests that they belong to the aristocracy of which Fragonard wants to highlight the **moral decay**. The story implicitly told by the painting quickly became source of humor and gossip, making the painting very popular. The figures' position form a love triangle set in an anonymous place as a garden, where aristocrats used to discretely neck, allows the woman to play an active role competing with the beauty of the nature, becoming its most dynamic element. Similarly to the woman's swing the viewer attention moves from a figure to another, from a symbol to another, following the visual story told by the artist. The masterpiece was commissioned by a noble aristocrat, probably the **Baron Saint-Julien**, who would have liked the scene to depict his woman pushed by prelate while the Baron himself should have been the man in the bushes. Fragonard accepts the challenge deciding, however, not to follow the Baron's instructions, rejecting any reference to real people and making the artwork a universal and timeless masterpiece.

26. PSYCHE REVIVED BY CUPID'S KISS

(Antonio Canova)

The story of Cupid (God of Desire) and Psyche, narrated by **Apuleius** in the *"Metamorphoses"* (II Century BC), tells of the astonishing beauty of the young girl **Psyche** and of **Venus**, who jealous of this beauty, sends her son **Cupid** to make Psyche fall in love with the ugliest man on earth. Cupid however, as soon as he sees Psyche, falls in love with her. Between the two starts a love story based on the condition that Psyche could not look at Cupid's face as humans were not allowed to love Gods. However, encouraged by her sisters jealousy who convince her that Cupid was in reality a monster, Psyche lights up a lantern to see his face while he is asleep. She remains enchanted by the extraordinary beauty of the God but, inadvertently, drops some of the hot oil of the lantern on his shoulder. Cupid then abandons Psyche flying away. The story benefited, over the centuries, of many artistic representations among which the sculpture entitled Psyche revived by Cupid's kiss, realized by the Italian artist **Antonio Canova between 1788 and 1793** and on display at the **Louvre Museum of Paris**. Sized 155cm X 168cm, the sculpture depicts the two lovers in a tender hug just after the kiss through which the God awakens Psyche from the eternal sleep she was "imprisoned" as a consequence of having violated Venus' orders and having opened the ciborium containing the secrets of Persephone's (goddess of the underworld) beauty. *"I'm foolish to be the bearer of such divine beauty, and not take a tiny drop of it for myself. It might even help me please my beautiful lover…."* - And with those words she unsealed the jar; but there was never a drop of beauty there, nothing but deathly, truly Stygian sleep. When the cover was lifted slumber attacked her instantly, enveloping her entire body in a dense cloud of somnolence. She collapsed where she stood, fell on the path, and deep slumber overcame her.

Photo Attribution, Wikimedia Commons, by Dinkum, licensed under Creative Commons CC0 1.0 Universal Public Domain Dedication.

She lay there motionless, like a corpse but fast asleep - (**Lumen, Western Humanities I, The Golden Ass, Book VI: 1-4 The tale of Cupid and Psyche: Ceres and Juno**).

After the awakening, with Jupiter's blessing, Venus forgives Psyche who joins the kingdom of Gods, becomes immortal and can finally happily live her love story with Cupid. Psyche's beauty hits so much Cupid that he loses his usual irreverence, becoming, through a metamorphoses that only love can generate, a tender e sensitive character. Psyche, on the other hand, symbolizes the human soul purified from passions and unlucky events, which gets prepared to live the eternal happiness.

Canova depicts Psyche stretching her arms and holding Cupid for the fear of losing him again, creating an image characterized by an unparalleled dynamic tension. Their fingers slightly touch their bodies capturing a moment which becomes eternal. Looking at the passive expressions of the faces it is clear that Canova, following the neo-classical principles, **consciously rejects the representation of any specific passion in order to elevate his sculpture to an ideal universality reaching a and compositional balance and harmony able to produce an immortal beauty**. All the elements, in fact, from the legs to the arms, from the wings to the rocks on which Psyche lays, express the artist's will to reach harmony and balance in the composition.

The sculpture, in white marble, polished and finely turned, was crafted using complex geometrical techniques which allow also empty spaces to have an artistic value comparable to the sculpted mass one.

In fact, the small space between the two figures' lips constitutes the central point of intersection of two diagonals which form **a soft and sinuous X shape** able to attract the viewer attention.

The detailed compliance with Apuleius' story is clearly visible also looking at the ciborium placed in the rear of the sculpture, which appears closed after Cupid let back in the smokes of sleep.

In addition to the famous Louvre sculpture, a second version of the masterpiece created by Canova itself exists and it is exhibited at the **Hermitage Museum of S. Petersburg (Russia)** alongside 15 more artworks of the artist. This second version was commissioned by the **Russian Prince Nikolaj Jusupov** who had tried in vain, on request of the **Russian Empress Catherine II**, to convince Canova to move to the court of the Empress

27. THE THIRD OF MAY 1808

(Francisco Goya)

"The third of May 1808", on permanent display at the Prado Museum of Madrid, is a painting by the Spanish artist **Francisco Goya** which **celebrates the Spanish resistance to Napoleon's army during the independence war**.
In 1807, after betraying the alliance with the Spanish King Charles IV, Napoleon orders his army to invade Spain, appointing his brother Joseph as a new King. The 2nd and the 3rd of May 1808 thousands of Spanish citizens organized protests and rebellions which met the brutal reaction of the Napoleonic troops that proceeded with thousands of summary executions. A line of French soldiers point their rifles at a Spanish rebel who lifts his arms in sign of surrender towards the soldiers and towards his destiny. At his feet the bleeding bodies of rebels just executed, while, on the other side, the scared faces, among which a praying monk, of the people who will soon face the same destiny. The city, symbol of civilization, appears far away in the background. With this artwork **Goya challenges the classical artistic**

Photo attribution: Wikimedia Commons, derivative work by Papa Lima Whiskey 2, pubblic domain.

depiction of the war which, through perfect proportions and ideal characters, was a mean to re-read history in propagandistic terms. On the contrary, in Goya's painting, both aesthetics and historical context remain intact and not idealized, managing to attract the viewers just by showing them the harsh reality of the conflict. Goya proceeds then to the **humanization of the heroes** which show no epic features, appearing instead like normal scared individuals before being killed. The rejection of the physical beauty as representation of the military heroism, however, does not preclude the possibility to depict it in a divine perspective. Looking at the painting from this interpretative angle, the man with the lifted hands from which the viewer can glimpse a stigmata (right hand), takes a position similar to the crucified Christ becoming, alongside all other rebels, a national martyr. The soldiers are depicted from behind in order to prevent any direct interaction between the viewers and bringers of death responsible of the horrors of the ongoing executions. **Goya shows the blood in a crude manner and with no filters**, marking a breaking point with other war painting of the same century, in which blood had never been depicted with this strength.

The light acquires also a crucial function in the painting separating the two groups. The rebels are illuminated by the radiant light of a lantern while the soldiers are left in the "darkness" of their actions.

The words of the famous art historian **Robert Hughes** sum up better than everything else these concepts: *"Most of the victims have faces. The killers do not. This is one of the most often-noted aspects of the Third of May, and rightly so: with this painting, the modern image of war as anonymous killing is born, and a long tradition of killing as ennobled spectacle comes to its overdue end."* In other words, the ability of the painting to attribute moral value to violent and tragic scenes became, since then, **the standard all other later war painting had to compare themselves to**.

A recent and suggestive theory questions itself about the meaning the blurry image of the two left bottom spectral figures, which seems to be mourning the dead, interpreting it as a self-portrait of the artist which would take form the bottom figure. This would demonstrate Goya's will to take part in the painting as a ghost added to the ghosts of the killed people, in order to honor their memory. Over the decades the painting has become more and more famous, being used as an image for stamps, postcards and book covers, acquiring the status of **symbol** of **the Spanish revolutionary spirit**.

28. THE GRANDE ODALISQUE

(Jean-Auguste-Dominique Ingres)

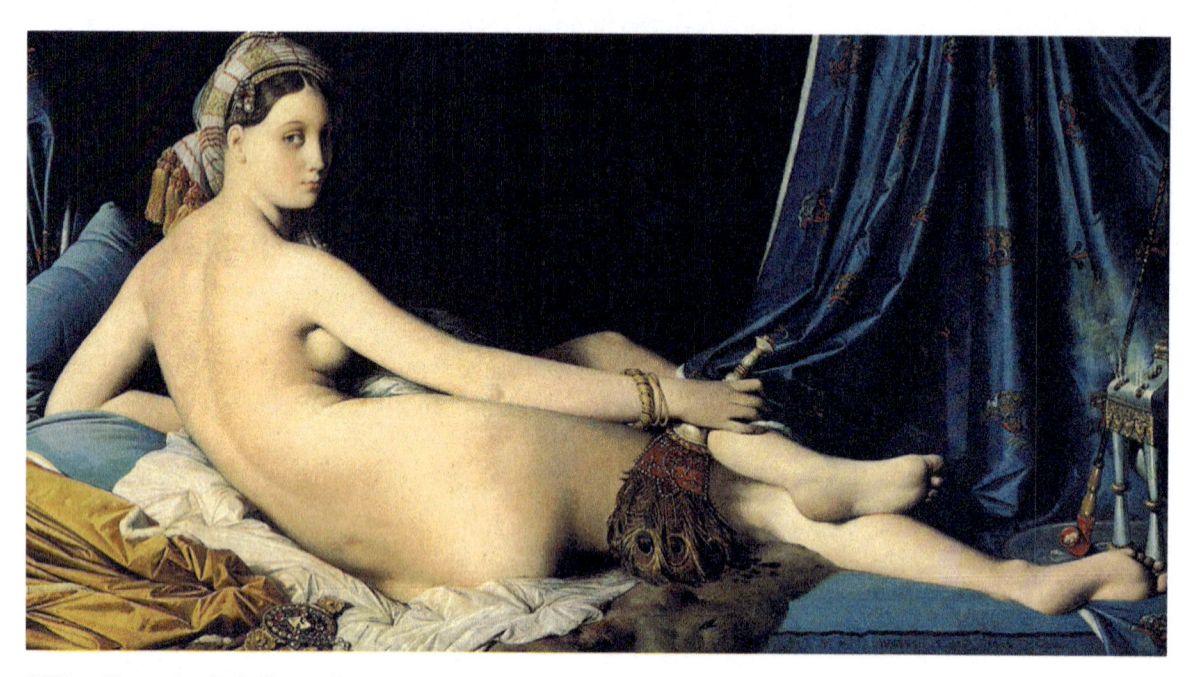

"The Grande Odalisque", 1814 oil on canvas painting (91cm X 162cm) by the French painter **Jean-Auguste-Dominique Ingres** depicts an odalisque, term originally derived from the Turkish word **Odalisk**, translatable as *"room assistant"*, which in XVIII century however assumes an erotic connotation, identifying the Sultans' concubines. It is precisely in this new evolved meaning of the word that the painting depicts, in what clearly looks a harem, the odalisque as a naked woman with a luscious attitude. The artwork was commissioned by **Caroline Murat**, Queen of Naples and Napoleon's sister, as painting intended to be placed next to another erotic work by Ingres entitled *"La Dormeuse de Naples"*, owned by Caroline as well and of which "The Grande Odalisque" has the same dimensions. The two paintings however were never displayed together as "La Dormeuse de Naples" mysteriously disappeared in 1815 after the execution of Carolina's husband, the King of Naples **Gioacchino Murat**.

Although the practice of depicting nudes of women was certainly not new for the art of that time, Ingres introduces an important element of novelty. Until then, in fact, nudity involved almost totally mythological figures being morally "accepted" exclusively by virtue of the idealistic function with which were conceived. In this case, instead, depicting an anonymous concubine, the artist totally rejects this paradigm. The woman, wearing just jewels and a

---

Photo attribution: The work of art depicted in this image and the reproduction thereof are in the public domain worldwide. The reproduction is part of a collection of reproductions compiled by The York Project. The compilation copyright is held by Zenodot Verlagsgesellschaft mbH and licensed under the GNU Free Documentation License.

turban, lays on her back forming a pink half-moon shape while turning her face towards the viewer and holding a fan in hand as symbol of wealth. On the right side is placed a shisha used to smoke tobacco or hashish, all set in a room decorated with fine damask and satin fabrics.

These oriental symbols highlighting the "distance" from France which, rather than the mythological idealism, represent the essential element of moral acceptance of the nude. The sensuality of the woman, although "detached" trying to hide her nudity, clearly emerge from the beauty of her body and face which seduces the viewer. An expressive contradiction which makes the painting mysterious and open to different interpretations. Moreover, in Ingres' conception, **sensuality and eroticism come directly from harmony of the woman's body shapes**. For this reason and to maximize the erotic impact of the Odalisque's shapes, Ingres resorts to some anatomical stratagems and tricks. For example, according to some recent scientific studies, the odalisque would have five extra lumbar vertebrae which twist her back and the pelvis, increasing the distance between them and the woman's head. This choice, according to some art historians, would also "hide" the will of the artist to highlight the distance between her thoughts, expressed through a detached expression, and her social role.

The painting reminds of many previous great artists' masterpieces: (1) the face is very similar to Raphael's *"Sposalizio della Vergine e dalla Madonna del Belvedere"*, (2) the framing *"from the back"* recalls Velazquez's Rokeby Venus and (3) the lying pose is in line with the artistic theme of the *reclining woman*.

The Moroccan writer **Fatema Mernissi** recently *(L'Harem e l'Occidente, Firenze, Giunti 2000, or Scheherazade goes West, or: The European Harem, 2000]*) pointed out that the Ingres' depiction of a nude woman, although the odalisques in reality were always dressed, is an example of the partial vision that the western culture had and keeps having of different cultures as the Muslim one. The painting is on permanent display at the **Louvre Museum** of **Paris**.

29. WANDERER ABOVE THE SEA FOG

(Caspar David Friedrich)

"Wanderer above the Sea Fog" by the German artist **Caspar David Friedrich** is one of the most important and celebrated masterpiece of the 1800's romantic art. In the foreground, from behind, a man with a stick wearing a traditional German green upper-middle class suit while, balanced on the irregular rocky surface of a mountain peak, enjoys, through the fog, the still visible features of a beautiful natural scenery. The landscape is likely to be the one of the **Elbe Sandstone Mountains** at the border between Saxony and Bohemia, which the artist re-elaborates turning it from real place into ideal place. The man recalls the artistic subject of the *"wanderer"* so dear to the German romantics, a sort of knight errant not heading to a physical place but, instead, looking for a place of the soul, in a spiritual and adventurous search within himself. His hair messed up by the wind symbolizes this inner torment as well as his need to find answers to the fundamental existential questions.

The two valleys, which visually meet on the wanderer chest, show Friedrich's will to put the human heart at the center of the painting and, with it, all human emotions, which often are mixed and contradictory.

The identity of the Wanderer, which some historians identify with the high ranking military official **Friedrich Gotthard von Brincken**, plays a secondary role.

Photo Attribution: Wikimedia Commons, Source: https://www.hamburger-kunsthalle.de/sites/default/files/styles/hkh_lightbox_full_wide_x2/public/ueber-die-sammlung-19-jahrhundert-caspar-david-friedrich-wanderer-ueber-dem-nebelmeer.jpg, public domain.

What counts is his function of **Rückenfigur (turned figure)**, an artistic tool which enables the viewers to assume the physical and psychological position of the wanderer, looking at the landscape with his eyes and immersing themselves in his emotional state.

Separating the man from the rocks just partially visible, there is a thick fog which does not allow the viewer to understand the right visual perspective, reducing his ability of comprehension of reality.

The painter wants to underline the limitation of human senses in the perception of the vastness of nature, recalling one of the fundamental concepts of **Kant's philosophy**. In particular, Friedrich refers to the **specific moment in which the limitation of human perceptive and sensorial abilities leads to the loss of his "power of judgement"**, intended as cognitive capacity of mental representation of reality.

As it happens for the seas, also in the case of the fog human beings can just imagine what lies beneath.

They become then aware of their partial abilities to comprehend the infinite, concept that in the romantic philosophy was identified with God and in the painting is represented by the fog melting with the clouds.

This intense combination of sensations and emotions is nothing but what Kant calls ***"sublime"***: *"Whereas the beautiful is limited, the sublime is limitless, so that the mind in the presence of the sublime, attempting to imagine what it cannot, has pain in the failure but pleasure in contemplating the immensity of the attempt"*.

Friedrich, by not showing the face of the wanderer, seems to be wanting to hide this contradiction between two contrasting emotions like fear and excitement.

However, this is not really the case as by overlapping viewer and wanderer the artist allows the latter to feel firsthand this inner contrast.

From a compositional point of view the artist paints in a vertical format in order to highlight the vertical pose of the wanderer.

The light seems to mysteriously come from below, illuminating the fog. Friedrich uses a mix of blue and pink variations in the depiction of the sky as well as in the depiction of the mountain.

Oil on canvas, 98.4cm X 74,8cm, the masterpiece is on display at the **Hamburger Kunsthalle Museum**.

30. LIBERT LEADING THE PEOPLE

(Eugène Delacroix)

Liberty leading the People" is an 1830 oil on canvas painting (260cm X 325 cm) by the French artist **Eugène Delacroix**, kept on display at the **Louvre Museum of Paris**.

The painting is inspired by the events following the **25th** of **July 1830**, date on which **King Charles X** of **France** proclaims the abolition of the freedom of press, the dissolution of the National Assembly and the institution of an electoral system in favor of the noble classes, generating the rebellion of ordinary people. For three days (July 27–29), known as *"Les Trois Glorieuses"* or *"Revolution of July 1830"* or *"II French Revolution"*, working class and middle class people start assembling spontaneously in the streets confronting the real army. The violent street clashes lead to the fall of Charles and to the coronation of the new **King**

Foto Attribution: Wikimedia Commons, Erich Lessing Culture and Fine Arts Archives via artsy.net, public domain.

Louis Philippe, the so called *"King of the Citizens"* who establishes a constitutional monarchy. Thanks to a combination of idealism and realism Delacroix creates a masterpiece which becomes symbol of this revolution. A female figure leads a group of rebels "dominating" the painting as symbol of liberty. She wears a red soft conical cap with the apex bent over (the bonnet rouge), ancient symbol of freedom from slavery, which had already been used during the I French Revolution gaining the status of emblem of the ideals of l freedom. The bare-footed woman, with uncovered breast reminding of the antique sculptures of Greece, the homeland of democracy, leads the people beyond the defense barricades erected by the real army, walking alongside the dead bodies showing the horrors of the civil war.

To the symbolic and idealistic meaning the artist associates also a modern e realistic dimension embodied by the French flag raised and waved above the head as well as the gun held with the left hand. The French flag flies also, in the background, on one of the towers of the Notre Dame Cathedral, conservative and reactionary symbol, to underline **the victory of change**.

The revolutionaries are depicted with extreme realism, representing symbolically, all the social classes who took part in the revolution. Their clothes remind, in fact, of different categories (working class, artisans, intellectuals, bourgeois and students) united by the pride of fighting for a common cause. The posture of the character wearing a top hat shows some hesitancy, the same hesitancy that initially the middle-class had shown in taking part in the revolution. The atmosphere, dominated by dark colors, looks very dramatic and able to reproduce as realistically as possible a scenery of civil war. Delacroix uses colors also to create an aerial perspective, also called ***atmospheric perspective***, namely a method of generating the illusion of depth which creates light through the contrast of dark colors with the brightness of the flag's red, without resorting to the representation of shades. The artist, who had taken limited part in the rebellion, left the explanation of the motivation leading to the creation of the painting to a letter to his brother Charles: *"if I cannot fight for my homeland......, I paint for it"*.

31. THE GREAT WAVE OF KANAGAWA

(Katsushika Hokusai)

"The Great Wave off Kanagawa" by the Japanese artist **Katsushika Hokusai** is a **woodblock print** (a technique of printing in which the image to be printed is cut out on a block of wood and then inked) of dimension 39cm X 26cm published for the first time around 1830-1831.

The artwork is certainly the most celebrated woodblock in the world, in addition to being the most emblematic and famous image of the Japanese art. It is part of a wider series of printing entitled *Fugaku Sanjurokkei* **(Thirty-six views of Mount Fuji)** by the same artist, of which the mountain is the absolute protagonist, being depicted from different angles, from afar, form nearby, in different weather conditions and in different seasons.
The Great Wave depicts a giant wave whose foam takes form of claws threatening to swallow up three fishing boats, in a scene of terror and struggle between man and nature which has as a background a snow-clad Mount Fuji, which seems to blend with the waves.

Photo attribution: Wikimedia Commons, The official position taken by the Wikimedia Foundation is that "faithful reproductions of two-dimensional public domain works of art are public domain".

Although the image has been considered by media, books, in t-shirts and even emoticons as symbol of a tsunami, recent studies revealed that in reality it is type of tidal wave known as **"plunging wave"**, a rare phenomenon caused by the overlapping of numerous wave trains. These waves, much higher than average, differently from tsunami suddenly break up before reaching the shore, losing their power in a relatively short time. The wave moves from left to right as an unexpected event, in clear contrast with the direction of the "predictable things" which in Japanese culture take place from right to left as, for example, in the case occurs in the case of writing. Artwork belonging to the Japanese artistic tradition **ukiyo-e (pictures of the floating world)** expresses, through the obsession for the Mount Fuji, the strong desire of the artist to reach the artistic immortality. The mountain was, in fact, considered both in the Taoist and Buddhist traditions the keeper of the secret of the immortality, as suggested by a popular interpretation of its name **"Fu-shi" (no-death)**. At the same time the floating world represents a "safe refuge" for the artist, who during those years was suffering from health and financial problems in addition to the grieving over the loss of his wife. Many see in Great Wave the **essence of the Japanese culture**, made of a compositional simplicity of forms which manages to penetrate the heart of the viewer.

It expresses also a meaning directly linked to the Japanese political, social and economic context of those years, in which was being taken in more and more consideration the possibility of **ending a 200 years period of isolationism**.

In this perspective of imminent change the artwork must be "read" a as masterpiece which on one hand communicates instability and danger and on the other opportunity and sense of adventure.

In confirmation of this, the painter uses the Prussian blue, a dark blue pigment known for its depth and durability, produced by oxidation of ferrous ferrocyanide salts which he had imported from Europe through China.

Being a print, there are many original versions of the masterpiece displayed in various museums around the world such as the **British Museum and the Metropolitan Museum of Art e Maidstone Museum (UK), the Art Institute of Chicago the Los Angeles County Museum of Art (USA)**.

The artist signed the artwork using the name **"Litsu"** adding the wording *"the previous Hokusai"*, in full continuity with tradition of the oriental art seeing the artists change their names as their career evolved.

The process of creation of a woodblock print uses a technique of absolute precision and accuracy which requires at least 10 years to be passed on. Despite the efforts made for its survival, today there are in Tokyo **not more than 25 masters (shokunin)**.

32. THE NINTH WAVE

(Ivan Konstantinovič Ajvazovskij)

"The Ninth Wave" is an oil on canvas painting (221 cm X 332 cm) by the Russian artist **Ivan Konstantinovič Ajvazovskij**, dating back to 1850 and on permanent display at the **State Russian Museum in St. Petersburgh**. The painting's title comes directly from an ancient nautical belief of a giant wave following gradually bigger and bigger waves. **Ajvazovskij** depicts, thanks to a technique of absolute precision, this particular scenario showing a giant wave getting close to some sailors survived to a shipwreck and clinging to what remains of the ship's mast.

The artwork best sums up the artist's attraction towards extreme natural situations in marine environments, which he exalted by attributing to the people involved the role of mere figures left to the mercy of the nature's will, in order to communicate the *pathos* characterizing many of his paintings. The restless movement of the waves and water's splashes further reinforce the impression of an ongoing storm, while the painting style and the colors used to paint the light gradually melt into the sea giving the viewer the impression of being inside the painting.

Photo attribution: Wikimedia Commons, source: Google Art Project, Google Cultural Institute, public domain.

The blue and green tones used to paint the waves express the survivors' feeling of despair and, more in general, the men's powerlessness towards nature, within a fascinating and at the same heartbreaking scenery. The yellow variations used to depict the light of the rising sun, on the other hand, open the door to hope, feeling which seems to prevail anyway over the imminent tragedy in which the survivors will probably be wiped out by the waves losing the lives.

Although the remains of the mast are the physical elements on which depends their survival, the sun's light that feeds their hope inviting them to resist becomes the fundamental message the painting wants to communicate. A clear Christian cultural footprint confirmed also by the remains of the ship which form a cross shape. One of the sailors raises his hand facing the wave in the hope of "defeating" it, showing the co-existence both of the awareness of man's role in the universe and his innate will to fight without giving up. In a romantic perspective, nature is considered beyond the realism of its depiction, becoming element able to generate conflicting emotions, as fear and hope.

The different combined artistic elements which compose the painting clearly contribute to make it a fascinating and dazzling artwork, able to express hidden meanings and symbolize the perseverance of the human beings. The artist's importance and popularity in Russia is confirmed by the words of the **Emperor Nicholas I** who, during a boat trip with the artist, said: *"Aivazovsky! I am the king of the earth and you are the king of the sea"*.

33. THE GLEANERS

(Jean-François Millet)

"The Gleaners", 1857 oil on canvas painting by the French artist **Jean-François Millet**, depicts three women, precisely three gleaners, intent to pick up one by one the ears of wheat left over from the harvesting while, on the background, other farmers are carrying out the reaping. The practice of gleaning, common activity in the XIX century's France, was considered as a lower classes' right to benefit from the unwanted harvesting left over by landowners.

Millet, through each of the female figures, depicts one of the three movements, particularly harmful for the back, which characterize the gleaning: bending down, picking up and getting back up. Rather than capturing a single moment, the artist, through the implicit repetition of gleaners' actions, manages to **"stretch" the temporal duration of the painting**. The women, moreover, appear so busy with work that they do not even look at the viewer, making him feel an intruder. Millet then created a sort of reality contained in a parallel

---

Photo attribution: Wikimedia Commons, source: Google Art Project, Google Cultural Institute, public domain.

world of which the viewer cannot take part but just look at. The artist resorts to the **Golden Angle**, of which Leonardo da Vinci had been master. This painting technique is linked, in turn, to the **Golden Ratio rule**, known also as *"divine proportion"*, which applies to art a complex mathematical principle that allows the artist to obtain the optimal proportions of the compositional elements of a painting and to place them in a way that exalts harmony and physical beauty.

In the artist's intentions the gleaners represent the whole French rural classes and the struggles that Millet himself had to face as a farmer, exalting their inner nobility through the image of the three women. In this perspective the painting becomes a tool, unknown to the French culture of that time, to denounce the **inequalities of the French society**. All this in a context where technological developments and economic theories had reduced the rights of the farmers compared to the previous system where the landowner had, anyway, a *"patriarchal duty"* towards the farmers.

The "cold" colors of the women's clothes contrast with the brightness of the piles of wheat in the background, separating them from everything around. The shades of the sunset, in addition, reduce the gleaners' chances of a good harvest, symbolizing a day which is already coming to an end. The contrast between light and darkness is also used by Millet to highlight the differences between abundance and poverty in the life condition of the different social classes. The sky itself, symbolizes the aristocracy which, from above, looks at the inferior classes whose place is the land. In the background, on the right side, from a "safe distance", a guardian on horseback monitors with indifference the women's gleaning. The dark traits of the guardian and his horse, alongside with the shadow behind the head of the closest woman to the painting piano, are the darkest points of the painting which move the attention of the viewer, placing him is a position of spectator similar to the guardian's one and making him an accomplice of his indifference. The artist, however, leaves room for hope thanks to the white dress and the blue and red women's head covering which recall the French flag, a symbol of revolution. Some experts underlined how the subject of the gleaners is also addressed by the **Bible** in the *Book of Ruth*, the Moabite princess who, in the XI century BC, after her husbands' death, abandons wealth and comfort to follow her mother in law Noemi and the destiny of Jewish people returning to Israel. Ruth is associated with positive values such as faith, good will and humility with which she carries out her work as a gleaner, elements which will lead her to salvation and redemption.

Millet's paintings (83,5cm X 111 cm) is part of the collection of the **Musée d'Orsay of Paris**.

34. LUNCHEON ON THE GRASS

(Edouard Manet)

The French painter **Edouard Manet** (1832-1883) has marked, probably better than any other artist, the **transition from realism to impressionism**.

Notoriously a rebellious personality, all Manet's works have a common main objective: **break up with French artistic academic tradition of the second half of the XIX century**. In this perspective, the "Luncheon on the Grass" represents the highest moment of the artist's rejection of the pictorial conventions of the time, opening the door to a *"new freedom"* from traditional subjects and forms of representation. For this reason many experts consider the masterpiece the actual **starting point of the modern painting**.

Oil on canvas (208cm × 264cm) dating back to 1863 and exhibited at the **Musée d'Orsay of Paris**, the painting was badly received by the contemporary critics who accused Manet of painting pornographic subjects.

The artwork's exhibition at the Paris Official Salon was denied and consequently it was

---

Photo attribution: Wikimedia Commons, source: Google Art Project, Google Cultural Institute, public domain.

displayed at the *Salon des Refuses* (Salon of rejected artworks). The problem was not with the female nude in itself, but with the fact that this nudity was not being shown, as per tradition, within a classical or mythological context.

For the very first time a female nude was placed in real and modern context. The woman chats with no embarrassment, looking at the viewers with full confidence, almost inviting them to take part in the scene. The two men, for their part, do not look surprised by the nude woman and accept it with great respect, not looking directly at her. The painting shows, normalizing it, the *"dark side of Paris"*, namely the one in which the sexual freedom defeats any rule of public morality. Furthermore, the Luncheon on the Grass, introduces the novelty of using **models belonging to the artist's close circle** of **friend**. According to some experts the appearance of the nude woman is the combination of the appearance of the artist's wife Suzanne Leenhoff and the one of his favorite model Victorine-Louise Meurent.

The man on the left is the sculptor Ferdinand Karel Leenhoff, Manet's brother in love. On the right, instead, the artist's brother Eugène.

Manet was also criticized from a strictly technical point of view for the use of points of color devoid of chiaroscuro, with no transition between light and dark.

The artist rejects also the academic tradition of the three dimensional perspective in place of a two dimensional one, which, for example, makes it look like the figures are floating in the air and makes unclear the borders between grass and water. Moreover, the grass is painted with weak brushstrokes with the objective of tricking the viewers and making them believe that the painting was not yet completed. As a result, the painting can certainly be considered as the starting point of a long and controversial artistic career aimed essentially at affirming a new and fundamental principle in art, namely **the freedom of expression of every artist**.

Pierre Bourdieu, distinguished French sociologist and philosopher, defined the Manet's work a **symbolic revolution** able to produce a radical change in the way people created, admired, interpreted and appreciated art. According to Bourdieu, Manet's art made a decisive contribution to create the world we today live in, which, precisely because is "ours", becomes difficult to perceive in its evolutions for us who inhabit it. In Bourdieu's own words: *"there is nothing more difficult to comprehend of what looks granted......since a symbolic revolution creates also the conceptual structures through which we perceive it."*

35. WHISTLER'S MOTHER

(James Abbott McNeill Whistler)

"Arrangement in Grey and Black Number 1", known to most as "Whistler's Mother", is an 1871 oil on canvas painting which certainly falls among the most famous portraits of the XIX century. On permanent display at **Musée d'Orsay of Paris**, it depicts **Anna Matilda McNeill Whistler**, mother of the US artist **James Abbott McNeill Whistler** who painted it.

The choice of the sitting profile pose, although had already been proposed in the past for other important artworks such as the *"Portrait of Letizia Ramolino Bonaparte"* by Antonio Canova o *"The Artist's Mother Seated at a Table Looking Right"* by Rembrandt, it is motivated essentially by the great effort that would have entailed for an old woman to remain standing for a long time. In a letter to her sister Kate, Anna explained *"(I) realized it to be too great an effort so my dear patient Artist (for he is greatly patient as he is never wearying in his perseverance) concluding to paint me sitting perfectly at my ease"*.

Painted during the artist's stay in London, the artwork, contrary to what many might think, was not conceived as a tribute to his mother. As its official title suggests, instead, the painting aimed at demonstrating, from a strictly technical point of view, the possibility to **modulate different grey and black tones to make them recognizable in twilight, through a perfect balance between light and shadow**. Then, as declared by the artist, the fact that *"everyone wants to reproduce their mother to make her look as beautiful as possible"*, has a secondary importance. According to the artist, art should be independent from everything else, it

---

Photo attribution: Wikimedia Commons, Musée d'Orsay, pubblic domain.

should place itself on its own appealing exclusively to the artistic sense of the eyes and ears, without confusing itself with extraneous emotions such as devotion, love, patriotism, etc. In an interview (1878) to the English magazine **"The World"** Whistler explains *"Take the picture of my mother, exhibited at the Royal Academy as an Arrangement in Grey and Black. Now that is what it is. To me it is interesting as a picture of my mother; but what can or ought the public to care about the identity of the portrait?*

The painting's color appears very soft, almost blurry, a sort of sigh on the canvas' surface which shows the ability of the artist of combining smooth brushstrokes with thicker ones. The woman's face and hands are more carefully painted being, differently from other painting's parts, characterized by more accentuated variations of color able to bring out forms and details. Anna wears a black mourning dress as a tribute to her husband passed away a few years earlier and which looks a sort impenetrable wall that produces a visual vacuity in the right-bottom part of the painting. Some shades of the wall covering recall Anna's face skin tone, while Japanese floral style shapes dominate the curtain in front of her. The wedding ring matches the golden colors of the frame which had been created by Whistler himself. Blue and red color sighs sneak underneath the silver and the grey, coloring the wall behind the woman. This play of techniques and colors generates a feeling of precariousness, made even stronger by the **perspective distortion** which allow shapes, including Anna's legs, to stretch horizontally making the viewers feel almost manipulated in what they are seeing. Hanging on the wall there is a frame containing another real Whistler's artwork entitled *"Black Lion Wharf"*, part of a series of 16 engraved prints depicting scenes on the Thames, inspired by Japanese art. **The influence of Japanese art** is also visible in terms of asymmetry (Anna is not painted in the middle of the painting), of use of ornaments, of dramatic use of colors, of gentle light effects and of renounce to an obvious creation of shade. Despite the artist never missed the opportunity to remind that his artworks sought only compositional harmony with no goal to convey feelings or emotions and that the identity of the depicted people should not interest the viewer, **the decision of painting his mother cannot be considered as a decision with no personal motivations**. Whistler paints his mother as an example of moral fortitude who patiently looks ahead probably thinking about the events of her life. The woman herself was very proud of what she called *"my painting"*, claiming it as an expression of her contributions to the son's career. The US masterpiece tour in 1933, in the darkest depths of the Great Depression, strongly contributed to make Whistler's Mother a symbol of strength, resilience and traditional values for American people. As a result, the image became a modern icon, mentioned in **Cole Porter's song "You're the Top"** and used by the US government to produce a stamp celebrating Mother's Day.

36. BAL DU MOULIN DE LA GALETTE

(Pierre-Auguste Renoir)

"Bal du Moulin de la Galette", also known as "Dance at Le Moulin de la Galette", is an 1876 painting by the French artist **Pierre-Auguste Renoir, part of the collection of the Musée d'Orsay in Paris**. One of the most celebrated impressionist artworks, the painting "captures" a specific moment of a typical social Sunday afternoon at **Moulin de la Galette**, a *Café* converted from an old mill with external space for dancing, located in **Montmartre district in Paris**. On the Sunday afternoons, in fact, intellectuals, middle class and working class, used to wear the best clothes to go to cafes and chat, dance, drink and eat the delicious *"galettes"* (savory crepes). The painting's atmosphere best describes the light-heartedness and the desire for happiness of the French people after the end of the **Franco-Prussian war (1871)**, anticipating a period of optimism, peace and economic development which will start with the so called *"belle époque"* (1880).

Renoir was one of the few impressionist artists to paint these social environments with out-

---

Photo attribution: Wikimedia Commons, Auguste Renoir - Dance at Le Moulin de la Galette - Musée d'Orsay RF 2739 (derivative work - AutoContrast edit in LCH space), pubblic domain.

door dancing, becoming undisputed master of this genre of paintings. In the foreground Estelle Samary, a 16 years old model wears a striped dress and behind her the sister Jeanne chats with the painter Franc Lamy. The man on the right, on the other side of the table, is Renoir's biographer George Rivière whereas the man smoking the pipe is the typographer Norbert Goeneutte. In the background regular people dance under some acacia trees and, at the same time, on the bottom left a child plays with her mother. To the viewer it seems a **live image** made of simultaneous actions, spontaneous behaviors, different pose and specific emotional moments such as laughing, flirting, friendly chatting, kissing and dancing. In this perspective we can consider Renoir as a **precursor of the cinematographic art** of which, his son **Jean**, great movie director of the XX century, will be master. It is worth highlighting also the effects of the light filtered by the trees on the characters' faces, on the land and on the colors of the women's dresses.

The poet **Stephane Mallarme** wrote about this painting: *"The strong daylight is filtered through the greenery, setting the blonde hair and pink cheeks of the girls aglow and making their ribbons sparkle. The joyful light fills every corner of the canvas, and even the shadows reflect it. The whole painting shimmers like a rainbow … the shreds of yellow, blue, and pink drift away in the breeze like so many butterflies."*

The scene, framed with figures cut out, gives the idea that it continues beyond the painting borders, which then represents only a part of a wider reality. Beyond the visual effects, the painting manages to transfer to the viewer also a sound dimension, enabling him to hear a continuous background humming made of laughs, chats and musing typical of amusing situations.

Despite the soft brushstrokes seem very rapid, the painting is the result of a **meticulous work of internalization and elaboration by the artist**, carried out through the transfer of the emotions felt on the spot into pictorial technique at his studio next to the Moulin..

37. A SUNDAY AFTERNOON ON THE ISLAND OF LA GRANDE JATTE

(Georges Seurat)

A Sunday Afternoon on the Island of La Grande Jatte", 1886 oil on canvas painting by the French artist **Georges Seurat**, is on permanent display at the **Chicago Art Institute (USA)**. The painting "pictures" the image of a regular Sunday afternoon in Paris: in a park on the banks of the Seine, women show off their fashionable dresses, kids play happily and different type of boats sail on the river. A modern image showing the different social cases mixing up and, at the same time, an image which still today remains mysterious as dominated by the **incongruence of space and proportions of characters**, who appear somewhat weird in their attitude and gestures. Every attempt to give to the painting a naturalistic interpretation has to be abandoned as the artist had little interest in the subject "nature" aiming, instead, at depicting a bright subject and a joyful composition characterized by harmony between horizontal and vertical lines. As Seurat himself told his friends *"I could have painted, in a different harmony, also the battle between the Horaces and the Curiaces"*.

The choice of a natural landscape as a background, so dear to the impressionists, should then be read as Seurat's attempt to tease them, as shown by the artist's provocative proposal to re-do their paintings in *"his own way"*. All the characters depicted, from the trumpeter to the man in black with the stick, from the couple looking at the child to the fishing woman, show no interaction among themselves, as if they belong to separate universes. The immobility of the figures is used a "tool" to denounce the **inability** of **the French society of the time to renew itself and welcome any type of change and innovation**.

On the foreground, on viewers' right side, a woman walks around a small monkey on a leash, very bizarre detail subject of much discussion by experts. According to some, the monkey would imply that the woman is a prostitute on leash, namely "at the service" of the man next to her. Others see in the monkey just the aristocracy's exhibitionism which, thanks to its wealth, could afford to do anything. In the middle of the painting a little girl, the only figure totally illuminated and who looks directly to the viewers. She seems to ask for help as well as express her fear for a future led by this noble class. In the contradiction of the woman fishing in elegant clothes hides, once again, the subject of prostitution, as if she is there to "fish" men.

Seurat took over two years to complete, at the young age of 26, an artwork for which he had produced many preparatory drawings and sketches in order to find the optimal perspective and proportions which could generate the high realism that the viewer can admire today.

The painting was certainly inspired by the researches illustrated in the book **"Grammaire des arts du dessin" by Charles Blanc**, who translates scientific theories on colors, visual perception and optical effects into a language comprehensible to the artists. As a result, Seurat uses a **new revolutionary pictorial technique** compared other contemporary artists. This technique, known as **Pointillism**, uses of small touches (points) of colors (in lieu of the traditional brushstrokes) which, through the optical effects of the mixing of colors, can generate brighter color tones. All this produces a **double visual perspective** of the painting: from close where single points are clearly visible and, from distance, where they interact giving the impressions of being united in regular brushstrokes.

Moreover, the painting is contained within an outline made of little points and by a white frame. The contrast between the colors of the contour and the ones of the painting sounds, once again, as a warning to the aristocracy and to his inability to see the needed changes.

The Island of La Grande Jatte is located on the western outskirts of **Paris**, between the municipalities of **Neuilly and Levallois-Perret**, a green area where today stands the financial district of *La Défense*.

Photo attribution: Wikimedia Commons, 1. cgfa.sunsite.dk 2. Art Institute of Chicago: database online: entry 27992, pubblic domain.

38. CAFÈ TERACE AT NIGHT

(Vincent van Gogh)

"Café Terrace at Night" is an 1888 painting by **Vincent van Gogh**. The masterpiece, painted live in **Arles** (Provence, France), depicts a scene having as a background the famous *Café Terrace* located in the old city and precisely in *Forum square*. Similarly to other impressionists, Van Gogh uses vivid and linear brushstrokes in order to reproduce what he can see from his workstation but, unlike them, he tries to express also psychological and spiritual elements strictly linked with his state of mind, confirming the therapeutic function that painting had for him. In a letter to his sister **Willemien (Wil)**, Van Gogh describes the masterpiece with these words: *"I was interrupted precisely by the work that a new painting of the outside of a café in the evening has been giving me these past few days. On the terrace, there are little figures of people drinking. A huge yellow lantern lights the terrace, the façade, the pavement, and even projects light over the cobblestones of the street, which takes on a violet-pink tinge. The gables of the houses on a street that leads away under the blue sky studded with stars are dark blue or violet, with a green tree. Now there's a painting of night without black"*. Basically, thanks to the use of contrasting colors, the artists manages to create a bright surface as a result of the internal light reflection which "defeats" the darkness. It is the first of a series night paintings by the artist, who considered *"the night is even more richly colored than the day, colored in the most intense violets, blues and greens"* and which will culminate with what probably is Van Gogh's most famous masterpiece, the *"Starry Night"*.

The painting's perspective allows the viewer to feel a passer-by who takes part in the scene,

---

Photo attribution: Wikimedia Commons, The York Project (2002) 10.000 Meisterwerke der Malerei (DVD-ROM), distributed by DIRECTMEDIA, public domain.

whereas, just as it happens in reality, the houses' details tend to become less clear and vanish in the background. The artist ignores the perspective vanishing points in some parts of the painting and follows them in other parts, as a demonstration of his **rejection of the creative limitation imposed by the traditional artistic conventions**. Van Gogh resorts to pronounced outlines to give form to the different figures depicted: people, tables, chairs, buildings. The stars' position is extremely accurate as astronomic research revealed that Van Gogh painted exactly the stars' disposition visible on the **16th and 17th** of **September 1888**, days in which he gave life to the painting.

The contrast of positive and negative emotions produced by the contrast of the colors is the main interpretative key of painting as clearly visible in many of its parts. For example, one of the elements that catches the eye, is represented by the contrast between the yellow, the green and the orange of the Café which express happiness and the houses' shadows which instead strike fear and sadness. The Café is considered as a *"salvation place"* and, according to many historians, should represent the refuge in religion as lifeline. The painter himself, in fact, had confided in a letter to his brother Teo to feel *"a tremendous need for religion"*. In this perspective has to be viewed the theory presented in 2013 by the researcher **Jared Baxter, who interprets the masterpiece as tribute to Leonardo's mural painting the "Last Supper"**. According to Baxter the twelve figures in the *Café* would be 11 apostles and Christ, while aside, on the Café doorstep, almost hiding, there would be Judas. *The Café Terrace*, today called *Café Van Gogh*, is still operating and welcomes thousands of tourists every year keen to feel the atmosphere and the visual perspective so magically depicted by the artist. The painting, an oil on canvas sized 80,7cm X 65,3cm, is on permanent display at the **Kröller-Müller Museum of Otterlo, in the Netherlands**

39. THE LADY OF SHALOTT

(John William Waterhouse)

The Lady of Shalott", oil on canvas by the British artist **John William Waterhouse, is a painting inspired by the 1832 homonymous lyrical ballad by Lord Alfred Tennyson**. Waterhouse completed three paintings which depict the protagonist in three different moments of the poetic composition. This review refers to the first of the three paintings, completed in 1888, depicting the **final epilogue of the story** and which is certainly the most celebrated of the three. The artist draws inspiration, in retrospect, from the **Pre-Raphaelite art movement** which between 1848 and 1853 brought together British critics, poets and painters opposing the Royal Academy style characterized by the promotion of rigorism and morality in art. Pre-Raphaelite painters, on other hand, believed in the simplicity and in the authenticity of the depiction of nature, following the Italian painters' style before Raphael, who was considered "guilty" of having idealized nature's representation, starting the evolution of the canons of beauty towards the standards of modernity. The story of the Lady of Shalott, identified with aristocrat lady **Elaine of Astolat**, unfolds as part of the legends of **King Arthur and the Knights of the Round Table**. She lives alone in the Castle of Astolat on the island of Shalott near Camelot and, due to a curse, is condemned to continuously weave images of the external world without looking directly at it. Elaine, on pain of death, is not allowed to look outside and her only visual contact with the external world occurs through a mirror pointing outwards the window.

No time hath she to sport and play:
A charmed web she weaves always.
A curse is on her, if she stay
Her weaving, either night or day,
To look down to Camelot.
She knows not what the curse may be;
Therefore she weaveth steadily,
Therefore no other care hath she,
The Lady of Shalott.

She lives with little joy or fear.
Over the water, running near,
The sheepbell tinkles in her ear.
Before her hangs a mirror clear,
Reflecting tower'd Camelot.
And as the mazy web she whirls,
She sees the surly village churls,
And the red cloaks of market girls Pass
onward from Shalott.

Photo attribution: Wikimedia Commons, The Athenaeum, public domain.

One day, however, after having glimpsed through the mirror **Sir Lancelot** on horseback, the Lady turns looking directly at him, thus violating the curse. The mirror breaks and Elaine, aware of the destiny expecting her but desirous of meeting Sir Lancelot, decides to reach Camelot by boat. Unfortunately tough, *"For ere she reach'd upon the tide the first house by the water-side, singing in her song she died"*. The painting depicts Elaine still alive in an expression of ecstasy and total abstraction of reality which seems almost pleading for the viewer's mercy while, on the boat, tries to follow her feelings despite the curse. The lips look half-opened as the Lady is singing a chant to help bravely face the unavoidable passage from life to death. The realism of the background landscape alongside its colors express the *pathos* of the moment and of the tragedy that is about to take place. The artist remains faithful to the poetic composition depicting the Lady dressed in white and sitting on a boat bearing her name engraved on the bow while taking her chains off, a representation of freedom from her physical and psychological prison. The white dress contrasts with the dark colors of the landscape emerging as symbol of purity, pain and sacrifice. Placed on the bow there are three candles, of which 2 have gone out and the other could go out at any moment, symbolizing her life approaching "the end". Also the leaf fallen between the Lady's leg and the edge of the boat represents life coming to an end, a life fallen and scarified for the desire of meeting Sir Lancelot. The cross, however, offers hope for the salvation after death. On the side of the boat is clearly visible a rug, made by "The Lady" herself, depicting with extreme care of details the live and colored scenes of the external world she would have liked to reach.

In the stormy east-wind straining,
The pale yellow woods were waning,
The broad stream in his banks complaining,
Heavily the low sky raining
Over tower'd Camelot;
Outside the isle a shallow boat
Beneath a willow lay afloat,
Below the carven stern she wrote,
The Lady of Shalott.

With a steady stony glance
Like some bold seer in a trance,
Beholding all his own mischance,
Mute, with a glassy countenance
She look'd down to Camelot.
It was the closing of the day:
She loos'd the chain, and down she lay;
The broad stream bore her far away, The Lady
of Shalott.

The painting, 183 cm × 230 cm, is kept on display at the **Tate Britain Museum** of **London**

40. THE STARRY NIGHT

(Vincent van Gogh)

Considered the queen of **Vincent Van Gogh**'s artworks, "The Starry Night", painted between the 16th and the 18th of June 1889, depicts the artist' powerful emotional interpretation of his view from the room of the **Psychiatric Hospital in St. Paul de Mausole (Saint-Rémy-de-Provence, France), where he had committed himself voluntarily**. The hospitalization followed a furious argument he had with his friend and colleague **Paul Gauguin**, with whom Van Gogh was sharing the famous yellow house in Arles (France). After the argument Van Gogh got so anxious that ended up mutilating himself by cutting off part of his own ear. The artist, therefore, gave life to the masterpiece during one of the worst moments of mental suffering, which unfortunately will lead him, the following year, to commit suicide. In the painting, elements that the artist could see from his window coexist with his memories and feelings, creating a powerful and complex imaginary puzzle.

In a 1888 letter to his friend **Emile Bernard**, Van Gogh writes: *"imagination is a capacity that must be developed, and only that enables us to create a more exalting and consoling nature than what just a glance at reality (which we perceive changing, passing quickly like lightning) allows us to perceive. A starry sky, for example, well—it's a thing that I should like to try to do, just as in the daytime I'll try to paint a green meadow studded with dandelions"*.

The sky occupies more than half of the canvas, with the rest occupied by the town and the surrounding hills. Clouds move vertically, stars shine brightly and crescent moon dominates the scene. The clear contrast between the peaceful town and the chaotic sky symbolizes **Van Gogh's emotional contrast**. The cypress on the viewer's left creates a flaming link between sky and earth which gives a sense of eternity and a surreal dimension to the painting. The bell tower, which reminds the style of the Dutch bell towers, expresses nostalgia towards the artist's homeland alongside a sense of greatness, isolation and loneliness. Both, the cypress and the bell tower, stretch to "touch" the sky as a manifestation of the **relationship between man and infinite**. The masterpiece marks also the evolution of Van Gogh's pictorial style, who seems to abandon impressionism in favor of a representation of reality where symbols play a crucial role. The outlined shapes are themselves tools of expression of emotions as, for example, the darkness of the sky which symbolizes the artist's fight to overcome his mental illness end the lighted houses which represent hope. Van Gogh's use of white and yellow creates a spiral effect which addresses the attention of the viewer towards the sky. Some historians, however, lead back the dominance of the yellow to the consequences of a lead poisoning of which the artist was victim of and which would have triggered a brain disorder affecting his perception of colors. For this reason then in the Van Gogh's last works colors become pure, violent, contrasting, with no shades and with no tonal alterations. It almost looks as if some for a magic energy moves the clouds through the terrifying vortexes of the night sky where only the stars act as fixed points around which colors and thoughts can gravitate. Ultimately then, the contrast of styles and colors feeds the contraposition between natural and unnatural, between dream and reality. Some art critics attribute to the painting also a religious meaning, thanks to what they think is a clear link to the old testament **(GENESYS 37;9)** : *Then he (Joseph) had another dream, and he told it to his brothers. "Listen," he said, "I had another dream, and this time the sun and moon and eleven stars were bowing down to me".*

This should represent Van Gogh's wish and hope that, after his recovery, his family could refer to him as an authority, changing their mind and their negative judgement (with the exception of his brother Teo) on Vincent's artistic career.

The famous song *"Vincent"* by **Don McLean**, a tribute of the American singer-songwriter to the artist, is full of references to the painting with its unforgettable refrain *"Starry Starry Night"*.

Photo attribution: Wikimedia Commons, bgEuwDxel93-Pg at Google Arts & Culture, pubblic domain.

41. THE SCREAM

(Edvard Munch)

"The Scream, painting by the Norwegian artist **Edvard Munch**, represents one of the most well-known artworks to the contemporary public. Standing before a boiling sky, flamed in yellow, orange and red, a blurry and wiggly male human figure with his mouth open, his hands on both sides of the face and his eyes wide open in sign of pain and fear, is depicted in the foreground. The figure's traits and expression could have been inspired, according to some recent and suggestive theories, either by a Peruvian mummy dating back to the **Chachapoyas** era (800-1200 AC) that Munch would have seen in 1889 at Ethnographic Museum of the Trocadéro in Paris or by another Chachapoyas mummy preserved at the Museum of Anthropology and Ethnology of Florence, whose resemblance to the figure in the painting is astonishing. The artist painted **4 versions** of **"The Scream"** between 1893 and 1910 other than a stone lithograph of which less than 50 prints exist. Our review refers to the 1893 oil, tempera, pastel on cardboard painting (91cm x 73 cm) housed at the **National Gallery of Oslo**. Two of the four versions are instead exhibited at the Munch Museum of the Norwegian capital, whereas the fourth was sold at auction for 120 million dollars in 2012.

In the composition of the painting, nature seems to take part itself in the man's pain without, however, having any consolatory function. Two men on the bridge and a boat on a fjord complete an atmosphere expressing heartrending anguish. With regards to the reasons leading to such an unusual mix of colors to depict the sky there are different theories: (1) the symbolic value of the colors, (2) the presence of *"Polar Stratospheric Clouds"* characterized by sheet-like forms slowly undulating (3) the 1883 eruption of the **Vulcan Krakatau**

Photo attribution: Wikimedia Commons, National Gallery of Norway, public domain.

of which the painter revised the spectacular effects it had produced. Certain is instead the source of inspiration of the painting, which should be attributed to a walk the artist was having with his friends in **Nordstrand (Norway)**, in a road opposite to a fjord with south-west view towards the sunset in winter months, when, suddenly, he experienced a strong panic attack, as the weight of nature and of the surrounding world was hitting him all at once. The artist himself describes this moment the 22th of January 1892 in his personal journal: *"I was walking along the road with two friends – then the sun went {I went} down, Suddenly the sky turned blood-red – and I felt a breath of melancholy – an exhausting pain under my heart – I paused, leaning against the fence, tired to death – above the blue-black fjord and city there was blood ‹in› tongues of fire. My friends went on and I stood there trembling with anxiety – and I felt that a great infinite scream went through nature".*
This implies that, **differently to what many think given the male figure's open mouth, it is the nature which screams and the male figure covers just his ears attempting to muffle the unbearable noise**. A real moment of dissociation from reality, an example of depersonalization disorder able to produce a disconnection from himself and the surrounding environment, almost like he was looking at his body from outside instead of being part of it. The episode represents the culmination of **Munch's mental suffering** linked to a very unlucky series of traumatic events he experienced since he was a kid. His Father used to verbally abuse him and the other members of the family. His mother died of tuberculosis he was just 5 years old and the same disease caused his sister's death when he was 13. Moreover, another sister was hospitalized in a psychiatric clinic. Munch himself wrote *"My father was temperamentally nervous and obsessively religious—to the point of psychoneurosis. From him I inherited the seeds of madness. The angels of fear, sorrow, and death stood by my side since the day I was born".*
In the attempt of expressing his feelings Munch abandons the traditional pictorial style based on the meticulous representation of the reality, in favor of a **new and unrealistic style**. In this perspective "The Scream" represents the attempt of the painter, through the language he knew best, namely painting, to express the trauma and the mental suffering that were tormenting him. More in general, today the painting is associated to the fragility, to the sense of bewilderment, to the anxiety and the feeling of precariousness which affect modern humanity and which made "The Scream" a timeless masterpiece.

42. FLAMING JUNE

(Frederic Leighton)

"Flaming June", 1895 painting (120 cm X 120 cm) by the British artist **Frederic Leighton**, depicts a young woman wearing a bright orange dress sleeping on a marble bench in a terrace overlooking a shiny sea.

She is turned on her left side with her head resting on an arm and the body in a crouched position, a pose chosen after hundreds of preparatory sketches and real simulations. The woman's pose was certainly inspired also by the famous **Michelangelo's statue called *"Night"*** which guards the Dè Medici's tomb in Florence, considered by Leighton the best western art masterpiece. The woman's identity is not univocally recognized even if most hypothesis lead to two candidates among the artist's models, namely Dorothy Dene or Mary Lloyd. Leighton artificially stretches the woman's neck painting her in a serpentine position which symbolizes danger and, at the same time, generates dynamic and almost liquid shapes on the dress, expressing **the depths of the subconscious and the dissolution of the body**. Moreover, the artist places on the woman's left side some **oleanders**, flowers with very poisonous leaves, in the attempt of highlighting the contradiction between the purity of youth and its potential dark side, a thin line between life and death.

It is exactly the continuous search of balance between opposite elements that constitutes the essence of the masterpiece. The upper part, in which alongside the relaxed expression passive shapes prevail, contrasts with the lower part, where the legs' positions communicates dynamicity and sensuality. The peculiar orange shade used for the woman's dress become the real protagonist of the painting, within which the body looks naturally dissolving. The artist paints 5 horizontal lines (sky, curtain, sea, bench and pavement) to counterbalance the vortex created by the dress.

Leighton objective is to give birth to a **unified artwork possessing intrinsic value**, with no pedagogic, political or moral aims. The ambition is to reach the beauty in itself which finds justification in the principle *"art for the art's sake"* which promoted the separation between art and any social or political dimension, inspiring Leighton throughout his career. The painting remained almost unknown until 1960, when, at the end of turbulent story, emerges as an absolute masterpiece. Gone lost at the beginning of XX century, it was found by chance in 1962 by a builder, hidden behind some panels of a fireplace in a house in London. The builder sold it to an art dealer for 60£ (British Pounds), who purchased it mainly for its big frame. The masterpieces was then noticed in 1963 by **Luis A. Ferré, director of the Museum de Arte de Ponce di Puerto Rico (where today is kept on permanent display), who offered 2000£ (British Pounds) to the art dealer as a pur-

chase offer. As explained by Ferrè's son, his father, being very aware of the great deal he was about to finalize, spent the entire night before the purchase in state of very high anxiety, worried that the seller could change his mind receiving a more advantageous offer.

43. THE SLEEPING GYPSY

(Henri Russeau)

"The Sleeping Gypsy", 1897 oil on canvas by the French painter **Henri Rousseau**, is today on permanent display at the **Museum of Modern Art (MoMA) in New York**. The artist himself describes the artwork in a letter sent to the major of his hometown **Laval** inviting him to purchase it: *"A wandering Negress, a mandolin player, lies with her jar beside her (a vase with drinking water), overcome by fatigue in a deep sleep. A lion chances to pass by, picks up her scent yet does not devour her. There is a moonlight effect, very poetic. The scene is set in a completely arid desert. The gypsy is dressed in oriental costume"*.

Rousseau, also known for his job at the French custom by the nickname *"Le Douanier"* (The Custom Officer), **started painting at the age of 40, keeping a style not directly linked to any of the artistic movements of his time**. Out of any predefined artistic scheme, then, the painting has to be interpreted as a post-impressionistic artwork in which emotions prevail on realism, a sort of poetic image of a dream. As stated by the French poet **André Breton**, Rousseau's art *"is painted poetry"*.

The woman, immersed in a desert landscape dominated by the moon, seems to be sleeping with her eyes slightly open, almost like she is in a state of perfect harmony between dream and consciousness. She does not look worried for the presence of a lion, whose behavior does not seem dangerous at all but, instead, almost protective, symbolizing as animals and human beings feel similar emotions. In this perspective the painting shows typical traits of the **primitivism**, a cultural trend "preaching" for the abandonment of modernity and the adoption of a new primitive life-style.

Although the woman seems calm, with one hand she holds a stick as if it could be an effective defense tool, highlighting the insignificant control that humans can have on their life. The woman, a musician wandering alone through the desert, represents the desire (founding element of **Realism**) of all people to live a life loyal to what are the personal inclination of each individual, something that modern society did not allow. Moreover, the fact that the painter depicts as a protagonist a confident and independent woman on his own, anticipates many of the **evolution of the women's role in society**.

All elements are painted very softly, except for the woman's dress which is characterized by "oriental shades" made through more intense and colorful brushstrokes. The masterpieces then recalls, in a poetic dimension, also the cultural movement promoting the imitation of the oriental world's way of living known as **"Orientalism"**. At the same time, from a technical point of view, The Sleeping Gyspy can be considered also as an anticipation of the **Surrealism** which, depicting unexpected elements (animals, people or things) within atypical pictorial compositions, aimed at producing a sense of wonder and curiosity in the viewers and at stimulating their inner feelings.

From a visual point of view many shapes are repeated as, for example, the horizon lines and the land line, the circle of the mandolin and the moon one, the stick and the lion's tail, generating what looks a "frozen" atmosphere where the figures become sculptures "embedded" in the painting. Moreover, the lack of movement allows the viewer to "witness" a precise moment in time and in the artist's mind.

The painting can also be interpreted in religious terms, identifying the woman with **Mary of Egypt**, patron saint of the penitents. In fact, after having wandered for years through the desert to obtain the forgiveness for her sins, Mary dies with lion next to her guarding her body. It is therefore a very complex artwork rich of meanings and symbols raising many unanswered questions, which are perfectly summed up by the Vietnamese poetess **Lam Thi My** in a poem dedicated to the painting::

Amazing night, mysterious desert moon, a young woman pillows her head on the sand, a lute, a simple jug of wine, does the woman sleep or dream? Desert night, a lion bends down and looks, touching the woman's hair, the night of his eyes is hypnotic, will the lion kiss the woman, or swallow her up? Is the lion a manifestation of time? Coupled with cruelty?
White desert night, black woman. Lute, jug of wine, abundant full moon, is this the riddle of naïve art?
Will the lion kis the woman or consume her? Who knows what the lion thinks? I understand, Henri, I understand
Cruelty and time will bow in homage, to pure, harmonious beauty.
Gentle desert night, a woman sleeps calmly, lute moon, jug of wine moon,
the lion bends down and looks

Photo attribution: Wikimedia Commons, by Oakenchips, public domain.

44. WHERE DO WE COME FROM? WHAT ARE WE? WHERE ARE WE GOING?

(Paul Gauguin)

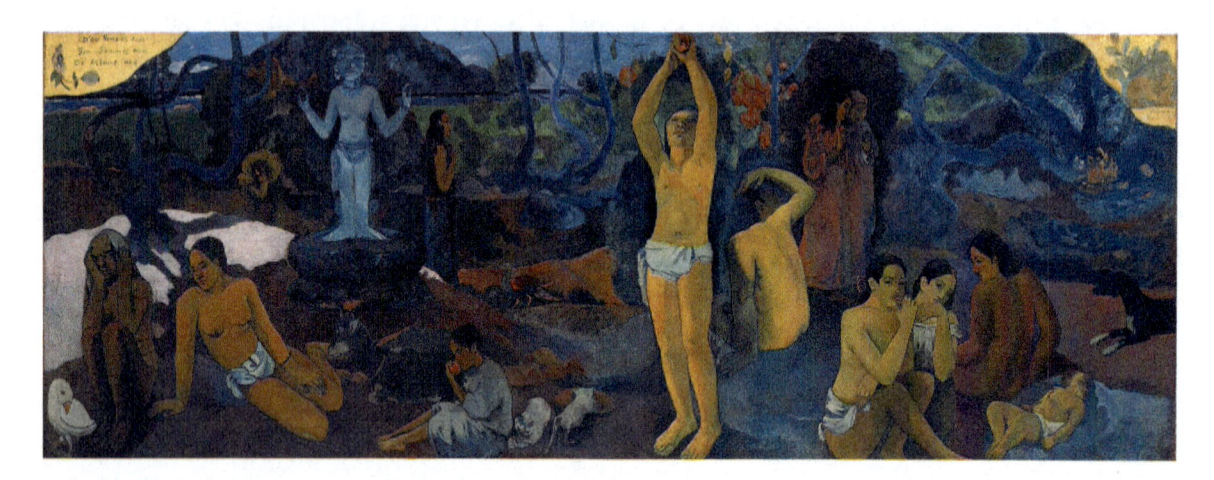

"Where Do We Come From? What Are We? Where Are We Going?", 1897 oil on canvas painting by the French artist **Paul Gauguin** is, by the author's own admission, his most important artwork. Through the painting Gauguin wonders and invites the viewer to wonder, about the three fundamental existential questions which make up its title. In a letter to his friend **Daniel de Monfried** the artist writes *"I believe that this canvas not only surpasses all my preceding ones, but [also] that I shall never do anything better, or even like it."* providing also a detailed description of the painting: *"it is a canvas four meters fifty in width, by one meter seventy in height. The two upper corners are chrome yellow, with an inscription on the left and my name on the right, like a fresco whose corners are spoiled with age, and which is appliquéd upon a golden wall. To the right at the lower end, a sleeping child and three crouching women. Two figures dressed in purple confide their thoughts to one another. An enormous crouching figure, out of all proportion and intentionally so, raises its arms and stares in astonishment upon these two, who dare to think of their destiny. A figure in the center is picking fruit. Two cats near a child. A white goat. An idol, its arms mysteriously raised in a sort of rhythm, seems to indicate the Beyond. Then lastly, an old woman nearing death appears to accept everything, to resign herself to her thoughts. She completes the story! At her feet a strange white bird, holding a lizard in its claws, represents the futility of words....So I have finished a philosophical work on a theme comparable to that of the Gospel".*
Returned to France after a childhood spent in Peru and countless trips around the world, Gauguin decides in 1895 to permanently move to the island of **Tahiti**, in the French Polynesia, where he marries a young local woman and brings the masterpiece to life. The creation of the artwork follows the death of one the daughters he had in a previous marriage and the

Photo attribution: Wikimedia Commons, Museum of fine arts of Boston, pubblic domain.

artist's attempt, luckily failed, to commit suicide by ingesting arsenic. As stated by Gauguin himself, during the suicide attempt *"I felt the need to paint a painting I had in mind"*. Through the painting, to be "read" from the right to the left of the viewer as an "evolutionary story", the artist depicts all the human life's stages: **birth, childhood, adolescence, adulthood and death**.

The three women and the child represent the beginning of life, the central figures the maturity and the hopeless old woman symbolizes death quickly and inexorably approaching. The single elements of the painting, however, keep their symbolic independence and have been, over time, subjects of interpretations not always univocal and based on the identification of multiple inspiration sources, contributing to keep alive the mystery around the deep meaning of the masterpiece. For example, the figure with disproportionate forms depicted from behind in the act of exploring the armpit, of which it is impossible to grasp the gender with absolute certainty, would represent, according to some experts, the moment in which humans comprehend their sexual identity. The man picking up the apple combined with the sitting woman eating the apple remind of Adam and Eve, of their curiosity and need to know. The fact that almost all figures are left alone with no interaction among themselves expresses Gauguin's attempt of going beyond appearances, giving a hidden meaning to the painting. In particular, through the solitude of the figures who seem to be living in separated worlds, the artist underlines the psychological loneliness of the human beings, who, from an emotional point of view remain still a mystery one to another.

The light, colors and the lines of the painting appear unrealistic serving as a tool to express the artist's emotions other than allowing to highlight the surrounding exotic landscape that he loved so much. In this respect, **Gauguin initiates the trend of "dismantling" lines and using color as a shape, which will be so dear to abstractionist artists**. In the background the perspective is generated thanks to the depth created by the ocean and the islands. With regards to the figures in the foreground, instead, is the distance among them to create the perspective.

In the masterpiece all the post-impressionist style of the painter emerges thanks also to the use of vivid colors and dense brushstrokes which express all his emotional charge.

The painting, (139 cm X 70 cm) is today part of the collection of the **Boston Museum of Fine Arts (USA)**.

45. THE ARTIST'S GARDEN AT GIVERNY

(Claude Monet)

"The Artist's Garden at Govern" (French town located in upper Normandy), 1900 oil on canvas painting by the French artist **Claude Monet**, is one of the most celebrated masterpieces of the artistic movement known as **impressionism**. Housed at the **Muse d'Orsay of Paris**, the painting depicts the garden of Monet's house whose care the artist had devoted great energy and passion to the point of defining it *"my greatest masterpiece"*. The artwork puts together Monet's two passions namely painting and gardening, as the artist himself

---

Photo attribution: Wikimedia Commons, TeNeues greeting card, public domain.

declared *"to owe to the flowers his passion for painting"*. Monet had worked for decades alongside his gardener to the creation of floral landscape where he could fully enjoy the beauty of nature and find inspiration for his paintings. *"My work is a slow work carried on with love and I cannot deny that I am proud of it. Forty years ago I moved this house and there were just a neglected farm with an orchard......I purchased it...step by step started to expand it and put everything in order...I dug, I planted plants and flowers".*

The artist's move to Giverny, which took place in 1883, is a watershed in his career and, more in general, in his life. Constantly in financial difficulties, Monet had always been snubbed by art critics, to the point that in multiple occasions he had to trade his artworks for meals and/or a place to sleep. From 1883 instead critics started showing much more in interest in Monet's art and his artworks began to be easily placed on the market, making him one of the most famous artist of his times.

In the painting, differently from other artist's artworks, the flowerbed limits produce an unexpected sense of order, representing **Monet's attempt to bend the beauty and the chaos of nature which he loved to his will**. Probably he was trying to control the evolution of events which in real life he could not control and which caused him a lot of pain and suffering such as, for example, his mother death when he was a teenager and the premature death of his wife Camille when she was in her thirties.

In terms of perspective, Monet draws a rather high horizon line in order to address the viewers' attention towards the picture plane, almost as if he was trying to project a new image to their eyes, an image able to catch, thanks to the use of weak and loose brushstrokes, **the impermanence of a specific moment of life**.

One of the key points of the impressionism was, in fact, to project the viewer to the specific moment the artist was experiencing.

Monet paints, in diagonal perspective, lines of iris flowers which thanks to the light filtered by the leaves of the trees assume different color shades. Although the violet dominates the canvas, the viewer can also glimpse spreading shades of red, gold and blue which melt with each other creating a perfect harmony. The results is that the viewer does not just looks perfectly at what Monet was looking, but, at the same time, is able to feel the scent of the flowers and hear the noise of the scene. **Monet's house and garden in Giverny are today an open air museum attracting, every year, thousands of tourist from all over the world**

46. LES DEMOISELLES D'AVIGNON

(Pablo Picasso)

"Les Demoiselles d'Avignon", 1907 painting by the Spanish artist **Pablo Picasso**, depicts, in a disturbing image, 5 prostitutes in a brothel located in **Avignon Street, Barcelona (Spain)**. Three of them have human faces while the other two have faces inspired by African masks which were much appreciated by the artist for their expressiveness, simplicity and stylized shape.

The masterpiece falls within the artist's **rose period** which starts in 1904 following his move to Paris. This period expresses, thanks to the use of bright and warm colors deriving from pink, Picasso's newfound happiness after the sadness and discouragement shining through his artworks of the previous period, known as blue period.

In the lower part of the painting the artist places a little table with some fruit (symbol of sexuality and fertility) whose disposition reminds of the male genitalia. The reference to classic concepts of painting such as still life compositions, always considered as symbol of the inexorable passage of time, reminds also of the transitiveness of human pleasure. In the upper left corner the artist places a hand which does not belong to any of the figures depicted and that seems to be holding up the entire structure in which the scene takes place, feeding into the mystery surrounding the painting.

Some of the over **800 preparatory works and sketches** featured two male figures in the painting which then disappeared in the final version. In particular, they were a sailor and a medical student that the artist in the final version move to the other side of the table, next to the viewer, participants of a scene of difficult interpretation and which strikes fear. Most of the experts agree that the sailor wanted to represent sexual desire whereas the student is the representation of **Picasso's fear of sexually transmissible diseases** such as syphilis which at that time was claiming many victims. The same fear seems to emerge looking at the sharp shapes of the women which express danger.

The women do not show any sign of interaction among themselves as if each of them belonged to his own world, addressing the viewers individually, calling each of them to define individually the feelings and the meanings that the interaction with each woman arouses in them.

With this masterpiece, that anticipates the cubist spirit of which Picasso will be maximum exponent, **painting breaks free of the artistic prison represented by the realistic depiction of nature, finding justification precisely in its ability to challenge realism through the creation of new styles, new methods and new techniques able to provide the viewers novel conceptual tools to interpret reality**.

Picasso rejects any distinction between figures and background, eliminating from his painting the depth dimension as well as the illusionistic creation of the prospective space. The painting, in fact, is based on a **two dimensional reality in which is possible to simultaneously look at multiple points of view**. To realize that is sufficient to simply look at the forms of the figures, shaped by the artist by including in a single body many viewing angles. The most evident example of this new artistic conception is represented by the woman in the bottom left of the painting, depicted from behind in a squat position with her face turned towards the viewer. The artist does not paint just what he can see in a specific moment, but also the information coming from his perception of what he is painting.

The women's poses and attitudes appear vulgar, rather direct and shameless, exclusively aimed at pursuing their own material interest through prostitution. In this perspective, the painting can also be considered a sort of starting point of the cultural evolution about the **role of prostitution in society**, contributing to encourage discussion on a topic towards which different sensibilities converge. On one hand the liberal vision which considers consensual prostitution like any other service provision. On the other hand the feminist vision which considers the men taking advantage from prostitutions almost as if they were rapists. The cultural debate still today continues, between countries which legalized prostitution and countries considering the purchase of sexual services an illegal practice.

The painting (243.9 cm X 233.7 cm) is on permanent display at the **Museum of Modern Art (MoMA) of New York**.

Being the artwork still protected by copyright, the image of *"Les Demoiselles d'Avignon"* cannot be reproduced in this book. We advise readers to type the title on an online search engine in order to visualize it on one of the many authorized websites.

47. THE KISS

(Gustav Klimt)

"The Kiss", 1908 oil on canvas painting (180cm × 180cm) by the Austrian artist **Gustav Klim**t, is on permanent display at **The Österreichische Galerie Belvedere in Wien**. The creation of the artwork follows Klimt's trip to Ravenna (Italy) where he had the chance to admire and appreciate the expressive power of the Byzantine mosaics, which will influence his pictorial style leading him, for example, to constantly use gold and silver in his paintings. The masterpiece, immersed in an atmosphere of passion and intimacy, depicts an embracing couple with the women awaiting for a kiss. On the man's clothes square shapes prevail as symbols of strength and virility, whereas, the woman's clothes are characterized by a floral style and soft lines representing femininity and maternity. This confirms the adherence of Klimt's style to the principles of **symbolism**.

The viewer cannot identify with certainty where on figure ends e the other begins, as love and passion unite the individualities within on single soul, a perfect balance of grace and beauty. Moreover, a golden halo surrounds the couple projecting it in a divine and infinite dimension symbolizing the **sacred value of love**. At first sight the man seems to physically dominate the woman but, looking more carefully at the exposed feet of the woman, the viewer can easily deduct that, if the woman had been depicted fully standing, she would be dominating the man. At the same time, although the position of the man seems intrusive, the way in which he holds the woman's head evokes tenderness and warmth.

Many experts also suggest the painting is actually a self-portrait of the painter and his long term partner **Emilie Floge**. However, with regards to the woman's identity, many doubts

Photo attribution: Wikimedia commons, Google Cultural Insitute, Google Art Project, public domain.

still persist as the artist was famous for his many lovers. Another hypothesis identifies the couple with the tragic **Greek myth of Orpheus and Eurydice as narrated in Virgil's Georgics** *(the story of Aristaeus and the bees)*. Eurydice, bitten by a snake in her ankle, dies in the attempt of escaping from Aristaeus' attentions. Orpheus, heartbroken for what happened, descends in the underworld and thanks to the beauty of his music manages to convince the underworld's Kings Pluto and Proserpina to bring her back to life, on the condition that Orpheus would not turn to see her until they reached the world of the living. Orpheus, however, breaks the agreement and turning towards her loved Eurydice loses her forever. From this point of view, the bare feet of the woman in the painting, would symbolize the re-emerging of the couple from the underworld whereas the kiss would just be a more romantic way to depict Orpheus' backward look.

The masterpiece is clearly influenced by various artistic styles: the use of gold recalls ancients *Byzantine* artworks (especially the ones in St. Vitale church in Ravenna), the garland of ivy leaves crowning the man's hair reminds of the classic myth, the composition links to the Japanese style, the contrast of the styles of the two cloaks is typical of the *"Arts and Crafts"* movement and the introduction of innovative elements such as new materials marks Klimt's rejection of the artistic tradition of his time, placing him within the new cultural movement known as *"Art Nuveau"*, of which the artist will be one of the most illustrious representatives.

The importance of The Kiss resonates to the contemporary times, a modern icon which has been used, for example, as source of inspiration by other artist as well as an image of a special 100 Euro coin issued by the Austrian government in 2003.

48. THE ENIGMA OF THE HOUR

(Giorgio de Chirico)

"The Enigma of the Hour", 1911 oil on canvas by the Italian artist **Giorgio De Chirico**, marks the **beginning of the metaphysic school of painting**. Metaphysics intended as ability to go beyond the objective appearance of things, which in painting becomes a tool to give shape to emotions and feelings. De Chirico defines the physical appearance of things as *"a moment, a thought, a combination revealing itself with the speed of lightning, make a tremble, throws us in front of ourselves as in front of the statue of an unknown God"*. **The truth of what people see then is not in the way things appear but in the enigma of the sensorial meaning that everyone attributes to them**.

The painter himself describes the revealing moment of The Enigma of the Hour in 1909 *"in a clear autumn afternoon I was sitting on bench at Santa Croce Square in Florence. It definitely was not the first time I saw the square. I was just recovering from a long and painful intestinal disease and was in a state of morbid sensibility. The whole nature seemed convalescent to me up to the marble of the buildings and of the fountains...then I had the strange impression to see everything for the first time...an enigmatic moment, because it was inexplicable.*

On the enigmatic nature of his artworks the artist will clarify in 1927 *"However, painting, with its material and hard-working side, keeps us as busy as the enigmatic and disturbing aspects of the world and of life. These elements enrich painting and make it worthy of existence; on the other hand painting allows us to show these aspects non just from an enigmatic and disturbing point of view but also from lyrical and comforting one; and it is right to be like this, otherwise we would be forced to withdraw in our workshops, in the warmth of our hearths and dedicate ourselves to pure meditation"*.

De Chirico's art is clearly linked to **Nietzsche philosophy, according to which animate and inanimate things have their own soul and language that the artist tries to express through painting**.

In "The Enigma of the Hour" the canvas is totally occupied by a building with a portico and arcades on a big square, while the empty space in the foreground is traced back, by some historians, to a chasm created by the removal of a statue's pedestal which could symbolize a tomb and then death. Three isolated and blurry human figures are identifiable: one dressed in white, one under the portico and a third one barely visible on the left side of the clock. The three figures are depicted in three different positions (from behind, in profile and from the front) as if they make up one single figure turning on itself, representing the circular dimension of time in contrast with the linear one measured by the clock which enigmatically reads 02.55, a time that seems not to match with the long shades suggesting a late summer afternoon. This contrast unveils the **coexistence of "different times"** in the painting which paradoxically contribute to make it a timeless masterpiece not linked to any specific moment. De Chirico puts the viewer in front an immobile time which creates an awaiting feeling of something about to take place and that nobody can predict. Reality becomes suspended in a metaphysic dimension that no clock can measure. In this perspective the masterpiece shows all the revolutionary power of De Chirico's art which, differently from other artists like Picasso who were looking for new ways to depict reality, aims instead at communicating, through visual art, a philosophic concept such as the metaphysic nature of time. Two different perspectives co-exist and interact in the painting: in the foreground figure the perspective is clearly centered whereas in the portico's arcades the point of view moves from right to left. The artist, using different perspectives in a context which appears normal and reassuring, proposes a vision of space made of multiple simultaneous points of view, generating a sort of uncertainty and disorientation in the viewer, showing him the existence of a fourth dimension, namely the metaphysical and unconscious sensation of time.

Being the artwork still protected by copyright, the image of *"The Enigma of the Hour"* cannot be reproduced in this book. We advise readers to type the title on an online search engine in order to visualize it on one of the many authorized websites

49. THE PERSISTENCE OF MEMORY

(Salvador Dalì)

"The Persistence of Memory", 1931 oil on canvas (24cm X 33cm) by the Spanish artist **Salvador Dalì**, is one of the most important and celebrated masterpieces of the **Surrealist art**.It depicts an unusual and weird landscape in which some soft pocket watches seem to dilate as if they were *"camembert cheese"* melting in the sun (definition given by the artist himself). The painting was influenced by **Freud's theory of the unconscious** and of the access to the human mind's hidden desires and paranoia, which Dalì had studied in detail in that period.

In the artist's own words *"the watches are nothing more than the soft, extravagant, solitary, paranoiac-critical Camembert cheese of space and time…hard or soft, what difference does it make? As long as they tell time accurately"*

The watch, a tool created to objectively measure time, nothing can do in front of the subjectivity of the perception and of the uncontrollable mechanisms of human memory. In this perspective, the painting becomes emblematic of the 1900's progresses both in science (Einstein's relativity) and in the comprehension of the human mind (Freud's theory of the unconscious). In other words, the artist wants the viewer to reflect about how the duration of time can "dilate" in the perception of the human mind, becoming elusive to any attempt to objectively mark it through a physical tool such as a watch. It is precisely for the impossibility to measure the human perception of time that the three watches strike different times.

The dilation of the watches along organic linear and amorphous forms immersed in a lunar landscape like the one of **Cadaques (North Catalonia, Spain)**, Dalì's homeland, symbolizes the artist's past, present and future. The stationary and immobile sea, once again, gives the idea of a time standing still and able to escape any attempt of being objectively measured.

The decomposition of the objective time in favor of each individual's subjective memory, perfectly embodies the artist definition of the surrealism as cultural and artistic movement which is *"destructive, but it destroys only what it considers to be shackles limiting our vision."*

One of the most controversial elements of the painting is surely represented by the white object laying on the land which, according to many experts, would conceal a **self-portrait of the painter**. To a careful analysis, in fact, the viewer can glimpse a nose, a tongue as well as long eyelashes covering closed eyes which seem to lead to a **dream dimension**.

The **swarming ants** on the only not-melting watch, typical element of many Dalì's artworks and traceable to a *phobia* he had since childhood, symbolize death and remind the viewer of the **impermanence of the human condition**. The painting is today housed in the **Modern Art Museum of New York**.

Being the artwork still protected by copyright, the image of *"The Persistence of Memory"* cannot be reproduced in this book. We advise readers to type the title on an online search engine in order to visualize it on one of the many authorized websites.

50. GUERNICA

(Pablo Picasso)

Guernica is a small Basque city (North-East of Spain), sadly famous for the bombing of the German and Italian air forces on the **26th of April 1937**. The military action, occurred during the first Spanish civil war, had the objective of supporting the military advance of the National-Francoists in the North of the country, at the expenses of the republican forces. The bombing was so violent that, in around three hours, three different raids took place, **costing the lives of over 1500 people and wounding another 1000 people**. The sky above Guernica took on the red-orange color of the flames while of the city remained just a burnt skeleton with around 70% of its surface destroyed. The report of the **Times' journalist George Steer**, who reached Guernica during the early hours of the 27th of April, describes the scenes of horror he witnessed:

"At 2 am today when I visited the town the whole of it was a horrible sight, flaming from end to end. The reflection of the flames could be seen in the clouds of smoke above the mountains from 10 miles away. Throughout the night houses were falling until the streets became long heaps of red impenetrable debris. Many of the civilian survivors took the long trek from Guernica to Bilbao in antique solid-wheeled Basque farmcarts drawn by oxen. Carts piled high with such household possessions as could be saved from the conflagration clogged the roads all night. Other survivors were evacuated in Government lorries, but many were forced to remain round the burning town lying on mattresses or looking for lost relatives and children, while units of the fire brigades and the Basque motorized police under the personal direction of the Minister of the Interior, Señor Monzon, and his wife continued rescue work till dawn".

Initially Picasso was commissioned by the newly elect Spanish republican government, the creation of an artwork for the Spanish pavilion at the **1937 Paris' World Expo**, which main subject should have been the technological development. The events of Guernica, however, shook up so much the artist's soul that, to express his emotions and, more in general denounce the atrocities of war, decided to give life to what would be his most political "contaminated" artwork, entitled precisely "Guernica". The masterpiece was completed in just three weeks, on time to be showcased at the Expo.

Immersed in a dark and sad atmosphere, the painting is full of images showing suffering people and animals. It is composed by just three colors (grey, black and white), the same colors of the newspapers which were the artist's main information source about what was happening in Spain.

Most of the images are also symbols: on the left a bull, traditional symbol of virility, becomes the representation of the brutalities carried out by the Nazi-Fascist forces. The bull is placed above a woman suffering for her dead child. In the center, above the remains of a dead soldier, the artist places a horse, symbol of the Spanish people and of its innocence, which appears in agony as a consequence of a terrible wound. The dead soldier holds a broken sword from which a flower comes out. On the palm of the other hand are clearly visible some stigmata, symbols of martyrdom. Above the dying horse, a flaming light which represents the bombs dropped on the city. On the right side of the horse a woman with her head and arm stuck in a window symbolizes a terrified observer. Another confused woman moves towards the center. On the far right a figure in agony screams while is engulfed by flames, symbolizing the innocent victims.

According to some interpretations, the warm light of the kerosene lamp held by the woman in the high central part of the painting, would represent Russia, one of the few nations to send concrete aid to the republicans in the form of guns, rifles, machineguns, tanks and planes. To Russia seem to look both the horse and the suffering woman in lower right part. On the contrary, the cold light of the electric bulb next to the lamp, symbolizes the indifference of France and UK, which preferred to remain neutral. Other experts see in the electric bulb Picasso's attempt of turning the spotlight and shed light on what had happened.

Other symbols of the painting are a dove (peace) whose body forms a shiny crack on the wall as symbol of hope, in addition to other hidden images such as, for example, a skull overlapped to the horse's body, a bull taking shape from the bent leg of the horse and some daggers acting as tongues of the horse, bull and screaming woman.

The story goes that Picasso, at the time living in the Paris occupied by the Nazis, met a German official who asked him *"did you create the painting?"*, answering to him *"No, you did!"*.

Over the decades the masterpiece acquired, in the people's imagination, the status of **timeless symbol of the atrocities of war, becoming an icon of the pacifist spirit**.

3,49m X 7,77m of dimension, Guernica is today on permanent display at **the "Nacional Centro de Arte Reina Sofia" in Madrid**.

Being the artwork still protected by copyright, the image of *"Guernica"* cannot be reproduced in this book. We advise readers to type the title on an online search engine in order to visualize it on one of the many authorized websites..

BIBLIOGRAPHICAL REFERENCES

RIACE BRONZES

Vlad Borrelli L.; Pelagatti P. (eds.). Due Bronzi da Riace, Rinvenimento, restauro, analisi e ipotesi di interpretazione, 2 vols. Roma, Istituto Poligrafico e Zecca dello Stato Publ., 1984. 396 p

J. Alsop, "Glorious bronzes of ancient Greece: warriors from a watery grave" National Geographic 163.6 (June 1983), pp. 820-827

Henrichs, Jennifer Alaine, "The Riace bronzes: a comparative study in style and technique" (2005). LSU Master's Theses. 2355

Raffaella Arpiani, "La statuaria severa: i Bronzi di Riace", Arte Essenziale, youtube video

RIACE BRONZES, Bulletin of the Institute of Classical Studies, Volume 56, Issue Supplement_105_Part_1, May 2013, Pages 541–554.

P. B. Pacini, "Florence, Rome and Reggio Calabria: The Riace Bronzes," The Burlington Magazine, volume 123, no. 943 (Oct., 1981), pp. 630-633.

Castrizio, Daniele. The Riace Bronzes. Recent Research and New Scientific Knowledge. Actual Problems of Theory and History of Art: Collection of articles. Vol. 9. Ed: A. V. Zakharova, S. V. Maltseva, E. Iu. Staniukovich-Denisova. — Lomonosov Moscow State University / St. Petersburg: NP-Print, 2019, pp. 67–74. ISSN 2312-2129. http://dx.doi.org/10.18688/aa199-1-6

Bronzi di riace: intervista al professore Daniele Castrizio, Classicult.it, 13 ottobre 2020, online.

Castrizio D. I Bronzi di Riace. Ipotesi ricostruttiva. Reggio Calabria, Iliriti Editore Publ., 2000. 32 p.

Michael Joseph Melen (Under The Direction Of Frances Van Keuren) B.A., The Riace Bronzes: Evidence And Support Of An Attic Provenance, The George Washington University, 2003

Dr. Jeffrey A. Becker, Riace Warriors, Essay, Khan Academy

NIKE OF SAMOTHRACE

Cara Grove, Unravelling a Samothracian Mystery: An Object Study of the Nike of Samothrace, The University of Warwick, 2018

Kevin Clinton, Ludovic Laugier, Andrew Stewart and Bonna D. Wescoat, "The Nike of Samothrace: Setting the Record Straight", American Journal of Archaeology Vol. 124, No. 4 (October 2020), pp. 551-573 (23 pages), Published By: Archaeological Institute of America

Andrew Stewart, The Nike of Samothrace: Another View, American Journal of Archaeology, Vol. 120, No. 3 (July 2016), pp. 399-410 (12 pages), Published By: Archaeological Institute of America

A.W. Lawrence, The Date of the Nike of Samothrace, The Journal of Hellenic Studies, Volume 46, Issue 2, 1926, pp. 213 – 218, Published online by Cambridge University Press: 23 December 2013

Hamiaux, M. 2001. "La Victoire de Samothrace. Découverte et restauration," Journal des Savants pp. 152-223.

Semiha Deniz Coşkun, tracing the trajectories of memory: the Nike of Samothrace, School Of Social Sciences Of Middle East Technical University, 2015.

Cole, S. G. (1984). Theoi Megaloi: The Cult of the Great Gods at Samothrace. (p.1-4). Leiden: E. J. Brill.

Louvre website. "A Closer Look at the Winged Victory of Samothrace"

Cindy Meijer and Branko van Oppen, Winged Victory, The Nike of Samothrace, Ancient World Magazine, 5 Giugno 2018 (online)

La Nike di Samotracia ci insegna che l'imperfezione è bellezza, a cura di Economia della Bellezza, 28 maggio 2020 (online)

Britannica Ecnyclopedia (Online)

VENUS DE MILO

Aicard, J. 1874. La Venus de Milo: Recherches sur histoire de la decouverte. Paris: Sandoz et Fischbacher

Pasquier, A. 1985. La Venus de Milo et les Aphrodites du Louvre. Paris: Editions de la Reunion des Musees Nationaux

Kristy Puchko, 5 Things You Should Know About 'Venus de Milo', MentalFloss (online), JULY 21, 2015

Philippe Jockey, The Venus de Milo. Genesis of a Modern Myth", in Z. Bahrani, Z. Celik, E. Eldem (dir.), Scramble for the past. A story of archaeology in the Ottoman Empire 1753-1914 (2011)

Kousser, Rachel. "Creating the Past: The Vénus De Milo and the Hellenistic Reception of Classical Greece." American Journal of Archaeology 109, no. 2 (2005): 227-50.

Andrew K, Iwanaga J, Loukas M, et al. (August 28, 2018) Does the Venus de Milo have a Spinal Deformity?. Cureus 10(8): e3219. doi:10.7759/cureus.3219

"What Was the Venus de Milo Doing With Her Arms?", World Weekly, 07 May 2015 (online)

OnurGüntürkün, The Venus of Milo and the dawn of facial asymmetry research, Brain and Cognition, Volume 16, Issue 2, July 1991, Pages 147-150
Branko van Oppen and Cindy Meijer Disarming Aphrodite: Rediscovering the Venus de Milo, World History (online) published on 08 May 2019
Britannica Encyclopedia (online)
Venus de Milo: The Oxford Dictionary of Art
James Grout, Venus de Milo, part of the Encyclopædia Romana

THE ARNOLFINI PORTRAIT

Erwin Panofsky, Jan van Eyck's Arnolfini Portrait, The Burlington Magazine for Connoisseurs Vol. 64, No. 372 (Mar., 1934), pp. 117-119+122-127. Published By: Burlington Magazine Publications Ltd.
P. H. Jansen e Zsófia Ruttka,y The Arnolfini Portrait in 3d: Creating Virtual World of a Painting with Inconsistent Perspective, , Journal of Scientific Computing January 2007
Benjamin Binstock, Richard de Koster, Venezia Arti, Why Was Jan van Eyck here? 2008
Harbison, Craig. "Sexuality and Social Standing in Jan van Eyck's Arnolfini Double Portrait." Renaissance Quarterly, Vol. 43, No. 2, 1990, pp. 249-291
Seidel, Linda. Jan Van Eyck's Arnolfini Portrait: Stories of an Icon. Cambridge University Press, 1993.
Celeste. Crowe. The Woman's Role in Jan van Eyck's Arnolfini Portrait, Journal of Undergraduate Research, 2019
Van Eyck's Arnolfini Portrait, National Gallery, official website video
Vicki Saxon, The many questions surrounding Jan Van Eyck's Arnolfini Portrait, ARTSTOR June 6, 2017 (online)
DR. Beth Harris And Dr. Steven Zucker, Jan Van Eyck, The Arnolfini Portrait, SMART HISTORY, (online videos)
Ritratto dei coniugi Arnolfini, Arte Opere Artisti (website), 10 Giugno 2018
Hannah Gadsby: why I love the Arnolfini Portrait, one of art history's greatest riddles, The Guardian, 17 Oct 2016 (online)

DEAD CHRIST

Life of an Object of Art, Lamentation over the Dead Christ, Silvia Minguzzi 2012.
Suzanne Boorsch, Andrea Mantegna, edited by Jane Martineau; London: Royal Academy of Arts; 1992

Johnston, Kenneth G. "Hemingway and Mantegna: The Bitter Nail Holes." The Journal of Narrative Technique 1, no. 2 (1971): 86-94.
"Mantegna, Andrea." Columbia Electronic Encyclopedia. Columbia University Press. 15 Mar. 2008
Starling, Dan. "Knowledge and Identitiy: Andrea Mantegna's Lamentation over the Dead Christ." (online article) 13 Mar 2008. <http://www.danstarling.com/page39.html>.
Corrado Mauri, Il Cristo Morto Di Mantegna, Scuola Domus Picturae, http://www.scuoladomuspicturae.it/articoli/il-cristo-morto-di-mantegna/
Federico Giannini, Ilaria Baratta. ll Cristo morto di Mantegna, capolavoro alla Pinacoteca di Brera, FINISTRE SULL'ARTE, 26/09/2018, https://www.finestresullarte.info/opere-e-artisti/andrea-mantegna-cristo-morto-pinacoteca-di-brera
Raffaella Arpiani, Mantegna: Cristo morto (Cristo in scurto), Arte Essenziale, Youtube Video

THE SPRING

Davide Lazzeri Concealed lung anatomy in Botticelli's masterpieces The Primavera and The Birth of Venus, Acta Biomed. 2017; 88(4): 502–509.
Debenedetti, A. and Elam, C. The Poetics of Painting: Botticelli's "La Primavera" & 15th Century Italy (eds.). 2019. Botticelli Past and Present. London, UCL Press.
Michael Rohlmann, 'Botticelli's "Primavera": zu Anlaß, Adressat und Funktion von mythologischen Gemälden im Florentiner Quattrocento', Artibus et historiae 33, no.17 (1996): 97–132.
Claudia Villa, 'Per una lettura della Primavera. Mercurio 'retrogrado' e la Retorica nella bottega di Botticelli', Strumenti critici, 86.1 (1998): 1–28,
Claudia La Malfa, 'Firenze e l'allegoria dell'eloquenza: una nuova interpretazione della Primavera di Botticelli', Storia dell'arte, 97 (1999): 249–93
CharlesDempsey, The Portrayal of Love. Botticelli's Primavera and Humanist Culture at the Time of
Lorenzo the Magnificent (Princeton: Princeton University Press, 1992), 3–19
Dizdar, Gorčin: Mediating Meaning in Botticelli's PRIMAVERA. In: Claudia Georgi, Brigitte Johanna Glaser (Hg.): Convergence Culture Reconsidered. Media – Participation – Environments. Göttingen: Universitätsverlag Göttingen 2015, S. 33–48.
Gombrich, E.H. "Botticelli's Mythologies: A Study in the Neoplatonic Symbolism of His Circle." Journal of the Warburg and Courtauld Institutes 8 (1945): 7-60.
Mirella Levi d'Ancona, Due quadri del Botticelli eseguiti per nascite in casa Medici (Florence: Olschki, 1992) 7–15
Botticelli past and present, Edited by Ana Debenedetti and Caroline Elam, 2019 UCL press
Nicole Lévis-Godechot, 'La Primavera et la Naissance de Vénus de Botticelli ou le chemine-

ment de l'âme selon Platon', Gazette des BeauxArts 12, 1 (1993): 137–48

Edith Balas, 'Botticelli's Primavera and the Story of Helen', Gazette des Beaux-Arts 137–8 (2001): 137–48

Museo Uffizi website

THE BIRTH OF VENUS

O'Malley, Michelle. "Introduction." Botticelli Past and Present, edited by Ana Debenedetti and Caroline Elam, UCL Press, London, 2019, pp. 7–9. JSTOR, www.jstor.org/stable/j.ctv550cgj.6.

Zambrano, Patrizia. "Sandro Botticelli and the Birth of Modern Portraiture." Botticelli Past and Present, edited by Ana Debenedetti and Caroline Elam, UCL Press, London, 2019, pp. 10–35. JSTOR, www.jstor.org/stable/j.ctv550cgj.7. Accessed 21 May 2021

Holberton, Paul. "Classicism and Invention: Botticelli's Mythologies in Our Time and Their Time." Botticelli Past and Present, edited by Ana Debenedetti and Caroline Elam, UCL Press, London, 2019, pp. 53–72. JSTOR, www.jstor.org/stable/j.ctv550cgj.9

Ventrella, Francesco. "Befriending Botticelli: Psychology and Connoisseurship at the Fin De Siècle." In Botticelli Past and Present, edited by Debenedetti Ana and Elam Caroline, 116-47. London: UCL Press, 2019. Accessed May 21, 2021. doi:10.2307/j.ctv550cgj.13.

Dempsey, Charles, "Botticelli, Sandro", Grove Art Online, Oxford Art Online. Oxford University Press. Web. 15 May. 2017

Hemsoll, David, The Birth of Venus, University of Birmingham, 18 min introductory lecture https://www.youtube.com/watch?v=-pzFEZwmDBc .

Ovadia, Eynav R., "The Venus Problem: An Examination of Botticelli's Venus and Mars" (2016). Student
Research Submissions. 67. https://scholar.umw.edu/student_research/67

THE LAST SUPPER

Grieve, A. (2018). The Scientific Narrative of Leonardo's Last Supper, Best Integrated Writing, 5.

Reflections on the Last Supper of Leonardo da Vinci, Jack Wasserman, Arte Lombarda, Nuova Serie, No. 66 (3), LEONARDO OGGI: Atti del Convegno: Umanesimo problemi aperti 7 (1983), pp. 15-34 (20 pages), Published By: Vita e Pensiero – Pubblicazioni dell'Università Cattolica del Sacro Cuore.

Pietro C. Marani, Leonardo. L'Ultima Cena, 2018

Ross King, Leonardo and the Last Supper (Walker & Company, 2012)

L'ultima cena. Leonardo Da Vinci. L'arte rivelata dall'alta tecnologia. Ediz. illustrata Copertina rigida – Illustrato, 31 dicembre 2012 di Domenico Sguaitamatti

Leonardo, Last Supper by Dr. Steven Zucker And Dr. Beth Harris, SMART HISTORY ONLINE

"After a 20-Year Cleanup, a Brighter, Clearer 'Last Supper' Emerges," The New York Times, May 27, 1999

L'Ultima Cena di Leonardo da Vinci: origini e novità del Cenacolo di Milano di Federico Giannini, Ilaria Baratta , Finestre sull'arte, 05/04/2021 (online)

BRITANNICA ENCYCLOPEDIA

SALVATOR MUNDI

Gutman Rieppi, N., Price, B.A., Sutherland, K. et al. Salvator Mundi: an investigation of the painting's materials and techniques. Herit Sci 8, 39 (2020).

Modestini DD. The Salvator Mundi rediscovered: History, technique and condition. In: Menu M, editor. Leonardo da Vinci's technical practice: paintings, drawings and influence. Paris: Hermann; 2014. p. 139–51.

B. Lewis, The Last Leonardo: The Secret Lives of the World's Most Expensive Painting (New York: Ballantine, 2019)

Marco (Zhanhang) Liang, Shuang Zhao, Michael T. Goodrich; Inverse-Rendering-Based Analysis of the Fine Illumination Effects in Salvator Mundi. Leonardo 2020; 53 (4): 380–386.

Jacqui Palumbo, Salvator Mundi: The most expensive painting in the world is getting the Broadway treatment, CNN, 3rd August 2020 (online)

Leonardo da Vinci and the mystery of the world's most expensive painting, The Guardian podcast. Presented by Rachel Humphreys with Ben Lewis; produced by Hannah Moore, Sam Colbert, Cheeka Eyers and Axel Kacoutié; executive producers Phil Maynard and Nicole Jackson, 31 Aug. 2020.

Alison Cole, How the Louvre concealed its secret Salvator Mundi book, The Art Newspaper 2020, The Art Newspaper, 2020, (online article).

What the Louvre's scientific examinations of the Salvator Mundi really revealed—according to the museum's own book, the Art Newspaper, Alison Cole 2021.

"The real reason why the Salvator Mundi didn't make it into the Louvre's Leonardo show", Alison Cole with additional reporting by Georgina Adam, The Art Newspaper, 7 April 2021, online article.

By David D. Kirkpatrick, A Leonardo Made a $450 Million Splash. Now There's No Sign of It, New york Times, 30 March 2019, (online article).

David D. Kirkpatrick and Elaine Sciolino, A Clash of Wills Keeps a Leonardo Masterpiece

Hidden, The New York Times, 11 April 2021 (online article).
LEONARDO DA VINCI-ITALY, https://www.leonardodavinci-italy.it/salvator-mundi

PIETÀ

Franco Russoli, 1963, All the sculpture of Michelangelo. New York, Hawthorn Books.
Giorgio Vasari, Vite de' più eccellenti architetti, pittori, et scultori italiani, da Cimabue, insino ai tempi nostri, edizione del 1550.
Bazin, Germain, 1968, The History of World Sculpture. Greenwich, New York Graphic Society.
Rizzatti, Maria Luisa. 1968. The life and times of Michelangelo. Feltham, Hamlyn.
Ziegler, Joanna E. "Michelangelo and the Medieval Pietà: The Sculpture of Devotion or the Art of Sculpture?" Gesta, vol. 34, no. 1, 1995, pp. 28–36. JSTOR,
Hale, J. R.. 1989. The Thames and Hudson encyclopaedia of the Italian Renaissance
Hartt, Frederick. 1987. History of Italian Renaissance art: painting, sculpture, architecture.
William, W. (1995). Life and Early Works (Michelangelo: Selected Scholarship in English).
James Hall, Michelangelo and the Reinvention of the Human Body Hardcover – May 11, 2005
Michelangelo. L'opera completa. Ediz. illustrata, 16 settembre 2013 di Frank Zöllner (Autore)
Michelangelo scultore – Illustrato, 15 gennaio 2006, di Cristina Acidini Luchinat, 24 Ore Cultura
Michelangelo: Marble as an Expression of Pietà, Marmomac (online), 2020
The Vatican Pietà by Michelangelo Buonarroti, VOXMUNDI (online), 2017
Ascanio Condivi, Vita di Michelangelo, 1553.
Berta Dröfn ÓmarsdóttirLa Pietà vaticana di Michelangelo, Analisi iconografica di un capolavoro del Rinascimento europeo, 2009.
William E. Wallace, Michelangelo: The Complete Sculpture, Painting, Architecture Hardcover – September 8, 2009
Michael Hirst, Michelangelo: The Achievement of Fame, 1475-1534 Hardcover – December 31, 2010
Gilles Neret, Michelangelo, TASCHEN's Basic Art series, 2016.
Antonio Piscitelli, La Pietà di Michelangelo è l'unica opera a recare la sua firma, ecco il perché,
2017, CONTROCONCILIO (online).
Michelangelo's Pieta, Italian Reinassance (online).

DAVID

Acidini Luchinat C. (2010) Michelangelo Scultore. 24 ore Cultura, Milano
Charles Seymour, Jr. "Homo Magnus et Albus: the Quattrocento Background for Michelangelo's David of 1501–04," Stil und Überlieferung in der Kunst des Abendlandes, Berlin, 1967, II, 96–105
Della Monica, M., Bernabei, P. A., Andreucci, E., Traficante, G., Paternostro, F., Peluso, F., Mauri, R., Provenzano, A., Giglio, S., Casazza, O., & Gulisano, M. (2019). Michelangelo's David: triumph of perfection or perfect combination of variation and disproportions? A human perspective. Italian Journal of Anatomy and Embryology, 124(2), 201-211. Retrieved from https://oajournals.fupress.net/index.php/ijae/article/view/10782
Saul Levine, Michelangelo's Marble "David" and the Lost Bronze "David": The Drawings Artibus et Historiae, Vol. 5, No. 9 (1984), pp. 91-120 (30 pages), Published By: IRSA s.c.
David Saad Shaikh and James Leonard-Amodeo, The deviating eyes of Michelangelo's David, J R Soc Med. Feb; 98(2): 75–76, 2005
Michelangelo "Il Periodo Fiorentino", Rai 5, Documentario
Giacomo Corti, Pilario Costagliola, Marco Bonini, Marco Benvenuti, Elena Pecchioni, Alberto Vaiani, Francesco Landucci, Modelling the failure mechanisms of Michelangelo's David through small-scale centrifuge experiments, Journal of Cultural Heritage, Volume 16, Issue 1, 2015
Rossella Lorenzi, Art lovers go nuts over dishy David, ABC Science, Monday, 21 November 2005
Povoledo, Elisabetta. "Who Owns Michelangelo's 'David'?". The New York Times. (31 August 2010)
Rossella Lorenzi, Michelangelo's David as It Was Meant to Be Seen, Discovery News, 2010
Mauro Di Vito, Selfie d'artista: il David di Michelangelo, Treccani Magazine, 15 gennaio 2016 (online)

THE SCHOOL OF ATHENS

RAPHAEL'S "SCHOOL OF ATHENS", Gertrude Garrigues, The Journal of Speculative Philosophy, 1879, Vol. 13, No. 4 (October, 1879), pp. 406-420, Published by: Penn State University Press
John Douglas Holgate, Codes and Messages in Raphael's 'School of Athens' August 2016
Haas, R. "Raphael's School of Athens: A Theorem in a Painting?," Journal of Humanistic Mathematics, Volume 2 Issue 2 (July 2012), pages 2-26.
Giovanni Reale, La scuola di Atene di Raffaello, Bompiani, Milano 2005, pagg. 65-68
Musei Vaticani online

Encyclopedia Britannica
Raphael, School of Athens, Khan Academy (online)
Arte Opere e Artisti, https://www.arteopereartisti.it/scuola-di-atene/
Scuola di Atene, Raffaello Sanzio, https://www.atuttarte.it/opera/raffaello-scuola-di-atene.pdf

THE CREATION OF ADAM

Alberto Angela, Viaggio nella Cappella Sistina, Milano, Rizzoli, 2013
Frank Lynn Meshberger and Md And Tony B. Rich, An Interpretation Of Michelangelo's Creation Of Adam Based On Neuroanatomy And The Use Of Symbol As A Metaphor Of Meaning, appeared in the October 10, 1990 edition of JAMA®, The Journal of the American Medical Association, Volume 264, No. 14
Rzepińska, Maria. "The Divine Wisdom of Michelangelo in 'The 'Creation of Adam'.'" "Artibus et Historiae Vol. 15, No. 29 (1994): 181-187
Pina Ragionieri; Miles L Chappell; Aaron H De Groft; Adriano Marinazzo; Michelangelo, Anatomy As Architecture : Drawings By The Master (Williamsburg, Virginia: Muscarelle Museum of Art, 2010), 36, 37, 55
Beck, James H. "Michelangelo's Sacrifice on the Sistine ceiling." Renaissance Society and Culture (1991): 9-22
Franco Bochicchio, La Creazione di Adamo di Michelangelo. Tra linguaggio artistico e saggismo didattico-pedagogico, Metis Journal Anno VI - Numero 2 - 12/2016
Stefano Di Bella, The "Delivery of Adam": A Medical Interpretation of Michelangelo, in Mayo Clin Proc, vol. 90, n. 505-508, 2015, DOI:10.1016/j.mayocp.2015.02.007, PMID 25841253.
Roger Porter, A Reflection and Analysis on the 'Creation of Adam' Sistine Chapel Fresco, Flinders University
Tranquilli, The creation of Adam and God-placenta, in J Matern Fetal Neonatal Med, vol. 20, n. 83-7, 2007, PMID 17437207
Wall, James M. "Controversy over the Sistine Ceiling." The Christian Century Vol. 104 Issue 24 (8/26/87 – 9/2/87):708.
Simbologia della Creazione di Adamo - Michelangelo - I SIMBOLI NELL'ARTE, ARS EUROPA CHANNEL (youtube)
David, Jeffrey. "The Sistine Restoration: a Renaissance for Michelangelo." National Geographic 176 No.6D (1989): 688-713

THE WOMAN WITH THE VEIL

Kaitlyn Greenber, Immortal Beloved? Raphael's La Velata And La Fornarina As Allegory, History, And Legend, 2018
Pisani Giuliano, "Le Veneri di Raffaello tra Anacreonte e il Magnifico, il Sodoma e Tiziano", Studi di Storia dell'Arte 26 (2015), 97-122
La Donna Velata, Portland Art Museum, —Jesse Locker Portland State University 2009
Raphael's La Donna Velata (c.1516) Simon Abrahams ,2014, EPPH
The arts post blog (online)
Analisi dell'opera (online)
Ars Europa Channel (youtube video)
Khan Academy (online)

THE GIOCONDA

Gernot Horstmann and Sebastian Loth The Mona Lisa Illusion—Scientists See Her Looking at Them Though She Isn't, i-Perception 2019 Vol. 10(1), 1–5
Al Moubayed, S., Edlund, J., & Beskow, J. (2012). Taming Mona Lisa: Communicating gaze faithfully in 2d and 3d facial projections. ACM Transactions on Interactive Intelligent Systems, 1, 1–25
Lorusso, S., Braida, A. M., & Natali, A. (2020). The Different Possibilities of Evaluating a Work of Art: Case Study of the Mona Lisa. Conservation Science in Cultural Heritage, 19(1), 307-326
Frank Zöllner, Leonardo's Portrait of Mona Lisa del Giocondo, Gazette des Beaux-Arts, 121, 1993, S. 115-138 (Reprint in: Farago, Claire J. (Hrsg.): Leonardo da Vinci. Selected Scholarship, New York u.a.: Garland Publ.,1999, Bd. III, S. 243-266)
Kington, Tom (9 January 2011). "Mona Lisa backdrop depicts Italian town of Bobbio, claims art historian". The Guardian. London.
See P. Rubin, `What Men Saw: Vasari's Life of Leonardo da Vinci and the Image of the Renaissance Artist', Art History, 13, 1990, pp. 34-46
A New Analysis of the Mona Lisa in the Louvre', Istituto Giapponese di Cultura in Roma. Annuario, 13, 1976-1977, pp. 23-35.
Jack M. Greenstein, Leonardo, Mona Lisa and "La Gioconda". Reviewing the Evidence, January 2004, Artibus et Historiae 25(50):17
A New Analysis of the Mona Lisa in the Louvre', Istituto Giapponese di Cultura in Roma. Annuario, 13, 1976-1977, pp. 23-35.
Liaci, E., Fischer, A., Heinrichs, M. et al. Mona Lisa is always happy – and only sometimes sad. Sci Rep 7, 43511 (2017).

Alessandro Soranzo, Michelle Newberry, The uncatchable smile in Leonardo da Vinci's La Bella Principessa portrait, Vision Research, Volume 113, Part A, 2015, Pages 78-86,
Clark, Kenneth (March 1973). "Mona Lisa". The Burlington Magazine. 115 (840): 144–151.
Nizza, Mike. "Mona Lisa's Identity, Solved for Good?". The New York Times. Retrieved 15 January 2008.
Debelle, Penelope (25 June 2004). "Behind that secret smile". The Age. Melbourne.
Johnston, Bruce (8 January 2004). "Riddle of Mona Lisa is finally solved: she was the mother of five". The Daily Telegraph.
Pascal Cotte, Lionel Simonot, Mona Lisa's spolvero revealed, Journal of Cultural Heritage, Volume 45, 2020, Pages 1-9
The Mona Lisa, The Secrets of Mona Lisa, Leonardo da Vinci Famous Painting Documentary, ART CORNER 2019.
Leonardo da Vinci: Paintings, Museum of Fine Arts, Boston, online video https://www.youtube.com/watch?v=YcLqoVRDPqw
Ulisse - Il piacere della scoperta 2017 - Viaggio nel mondo della Gioconda, Trasmissione Rai Uno condotta da Alberto Angela 2017.
ALBERTO ANGELA: IL SEGRETO DELLA GIOCONDA, Givediscienza 2016, online video https://www.youtube.com/watch?v=4mp_RZP9WbE&t=59s

VENUS OF URBIN

VEILING THE "VENUS OF URBINO", Mary Pardo, 1997, Titian's "Venus of Urbino".
UFFIZI ONLINE
ARTSY "Venus of Urbino" Titian's Iconic Painting, Explained, Sarah Dotson 2020
SINGUALART Venus of Urbino (1534): The Story Behind Titian's Controversial Painting, TARA LLOYD
WIDEWALLS, Venus of Urbino, Titian's Most Sensual Painting, Balasz Takac 2020
The guardian, He was one of the greatest of all Venetian artists, but who was Giorgione? 2016 John-Paul Stonard
UNIVERSITY OF CINCINNATI 2007c, Catherine L. Yellig, Rethinking the Renaissance Courtesan: Contemporary Interpretation of Three Paintings by Titian (Tiziano Vecellio 1485 – 1576)

BASKET OF FRUIT

Michelangelo Merisi da Caravaggio (1571–1610).Basket of Fruit (1596), P. Potter ,NCBI, 2003

The Instrument of Caravaggio, Antonino Saggio, 2010
Canestra di frutta. Caravaggio. Collana: I capolavori dell'arte, n. 2; Autore/Curatore: Philippe Daverio. Editore: Corriere della Sera, 2020.
Caravaggio segreto. I misteri nascosti nei suoi capolavoriAutore, Costantino D'Orazio, Editore: Sperling & KupferCollana: Pickwick, 2014
Caravaggio's Fruit: A Mirror on Baroque Horticulture, Jules Janick, Chronica Horticulturae A Publication Of The International Society For Horticultural Science Volume 44 - Number 4 - 2004
Basket of fruit, Michelangelo Merisi da Caravaggio (1571-1610), Ambrosiana (online)
A Closer Look at Basket of Fruit by Michelangelo Caravaggio Dan Scott, August 4 2020 (online)
Caravaggio, Lectio Magistralis di Vittorio Sgarbi, a Incontrarsi a Salsomaggiore (youtube video)
Caravaggio a Geo e Geo - Segreti spiegati da Costantino D'Orazio (Rai3)
Canestra di frutta di Caravaggio: analisi completa dell'opera, Dario Mastromattei, ARTE-WORLD, pubblicato 15 giugno 2015 · aggiornato 22 febbraio 2017 (ONLINE)
Still life Caravaggio: Caravaggio's Basket of Fruit, THE ART SPOT BLOG, Monday April 3rd 2017 (ONLINE)

ECCE HOMO

La Repubblica
La Stampa
Raiplay
The Guardian
Wikipedia
El Pais
La Nuova Sardegna
ARS MAGAZINE, Entervista a Nicola Spinosa, https://arsmagazine.com/entrevista-a-nicola-spinosa/

APOLLO E DAFNE

Desiderio and Diletto: Vision, Touch and the Poetics of Bernini's Apollo and Daphne, Andrea Bolland, The Art Bulletin, Vol. 82, No. 2 (Jun., 2000), pp. 309-330 (22 pages) Published By: CAA

Alessandro Barchiesi, Metamorfosi vol. I (Libri I-II), 2019, Fondazione lorenzo Vall - Arnoldo mondadori editore.
Bernini's metamorphosis: sculpture, poetry, and the embodied beholder J. Joris van Gastel, Word & Image, Volume 28, 2012 - Issue 2, Pages 193-205 | Published online: 30 Jul 2012
Genevieve Warwick, Speaking Statues: Bernini's Apollo and Daphne at the Villa Borghese, June 2004, Art History 27(3)
Simon Schama, When stone came to life, The Guardian (online), Sat 16 Sep 2006.
Motion as Lust in Bernini's Apollo and Daphne, by Daniel Whitten, Lebanon Valley College
Apollo and Daphne: A Tale of Cupid's Revenge Told by Ovid and Bernini by Ruben Cordova February 8, 2021, glasstire.com
Lavin, Irving. Bernini and the Unity of the Visual Arts. For Pierpont Morgan Library by Oxford University Press, 1980
Gian Lorenzo Bernini, Apollo and Daphne, A conversation with Dr. Beth Harris and Dr. Steven Zucker, Smart History video, https://www.youtube.com/watch?v=bdnPdZMZ9PU.
Apollo and Daphne, The Artble (online)

THE CONSEQUENCES OF WAR

On The Consequences Of The War, Katarina Chmelinova, Quart 2014
Smart History
Khan Academy
The Consequences of War -Peter Paul Rubens March 11, 2019 by Kelly Bagdanov
Mark Lamster is the author of "Master of Shadows: The Secret Diplomatic Career of the Painter Peter Paul Rubens, 2010.
Amy Florence, Canvas Magazine (online)
Museo degli Uffizi (Online)

THE NIGHT WATCH

Esther Van Duijn, The Art of Conservation III: The Restorations of Rembrandt's 'Night Watch, 2016, The Burlington Magazine
Gary Schwart, The Rembrandt Book Hardcover, 2019
María Castañeda-Delgado, Becoming-Artwork: Rethinking Agency and Performativity Through the Conservation History of Rembrandt's The Night Watch (1642), Concordia University, 2020
Dr. Wendy Schaller, "Rembrandt, The Night Watch," in Smarthistory, August 8, 2015.

Unravelling the riddle of Rembrandt's The Night Watch, Christie's, 2019

The Night Watch, Rembrandt van Rijn, 1642, RIJKSMUSEUM (online painting descrition)

Why Rembrandt's The Night Watch is still a mystery, BBC, Fisun Güner, 2019

Dario Mastromattei, La Ronda di notte di Rembrandt: la foto di gruppo più famosa della storia, ARTEWORLD (Online), 2013

Kristy Puchko, 16 Things You Might Not Know About Rembrandt's The Night Watch, 2015

Experience the Night Watch, https://beleefdenachtwacht.nl/en .

Theresa Machemer, Explore a Hyper-Resolution Rendering of Rembrandt's 'The Night Watch' Online, smithsonianmag.com, 2020

Nancy Kenney, Trimmed, splashed and slashed: the anatomy of Rembrandt's The Night Watch, The art news paper, 2019.

Zuzanna Stanska, 15 Things You May Not Know About The Night Watch by Rembrandt, The Daily Art Magazine, 2019

Britannica Encyclopedia

LAS MENINAS

Ione, Amy. (2008). Las Meninas: Examining Velasquez's Enigmatic Painting. Journal of Consciousness Studies. 15.

Byron Hamann, The Mirrors of Las Meninas: Cochineal, Silver, and Clay, The Art Bulletin, Volume XXCII, numbers 1-2, March – June 2010

Charles de Tolnay, "Velazquez' Las Hilanderas and Las Meninas," GBA, 35, 1949,. 21-38.

Editorial (January 1985). "The cleaning of 'Las Meninas'". The Burlington Magazine. Burlington Magazine Publications Ltd. 127 (982): 2–3, 41.

Kubler, George (1966). "Three Remarks on the Meninas". The Art Bulletin. 48 (2): 212–214.

Brown, Jonathan and Garrido, Carmen (1998), Velázquez: The Technique of Genius (New Haven and London: Yale University Press).

Elkins, James (1999), Why Are Our Pictures Puzzles: On the Modern Origins of Pictorial Complexity (New York and London: Routledge).

Foucault, Michel (1970), The Order of Things (New York: Random House). Kahr, Madlyn Millner (1976), Velazquez: The Art of Painting (New York: Harper & Row, Publishers).

Steinberg, Leo (1981), 'Velásquez' Las Meninas', October, 19, pp. 45–54. Tyler, Christopher W. (1998), 'Painters centre one eye in portraits', Nature, 392,pp. 877–78.

"Diego Velázquez, Las Meninas". ColourLex. Archived from the original on 31 July 2015. Retrieved 19 March 2021.

Leppanen, Analisa (2000). "Into the house of mirrors: the carnivalesque in Las Meninas". Aurora. 1. page numbers unknown

Tyler, C.W. (2007), 'Some principles of spatial organization in art', Spatial Vision, 20 (6), pp. 509–30.

THE GIRL WITH THE PEARL EARRING

Tracy Chevalier Girl With a Pearl Earring, , HarperCollins Publishers, 2006
"Revealing the painterly technique beneath the surface of Vermeer's Girl with a Pearl Earring using macro- and microscale imaging" by Abbie Vandivere, Annelies van Loon, Kathryn A. Dooley, Ralph Haswell, Robert G. Erdmann, Emilien Leonhardt & John K. Delaney, Heritage Science, 2019
The Girl in the Spotlight: Vermeer at work, his materials and techniques in Girl with a Pearl Earring, Abbie Vandivere, Jørgen Wadum & Emilien Leonhardt, Heritage Science 2020
From 'Vermeer Illuminated' to 'The Girl in the Spotlight': approaches and methodologies for the scientific (re-)examination of Vermeer's Girl with a Pearl Earring
Abbie Vandivere, Jørgen Wadum, Klaas Jan van den Berg, Annelies van Loon & The Girl in the Spotlight research team, Heritage Science, 2019.
Gaskell I, Jonker M, editors. Vermeer studies: studies in the history of art 55. National Gallery of Art Washington: New Haven; 1988.
Groen K, van der Werf I, van den Berg K, Boon J. Scientifc examination
of Vermeer's "Girl with a Pearl Earring". In: Gaskell I, Jonker M, editors.
Vermeer studies: studies in the history of art 55. New Haven: National Gallery of Art, Washington; 1988. p. 168–83.
James Earle, Why is Vermeer's "Girl with the Pearl Earring" considered a masterpiece?, TEDed video
Vermeer Beyond Time (DVD) directors: Jean-Pierre Cottet, Guillaume Cottet, 2017
Britannica Encyclopedia

THE LACEMAKER

KK Filipczak, Zirka Z. "Vermeer, Elusiveness, and Visual Theory." Simiolus: Netherlands Quarterly for the History of Art 32, no. 4 (2006): 259-72
Vermeer studies: studies in the history of art 55. New Haven: National Gallery of Art, Washington; 1988. p. 168–83.
Liedtke, Walter; Johnson, C. Richard, Jr.; Johnson, Don H. "Canvas matches in Vermeer: a case study in the computer analysis of canvas supports".
Vermeer Beyond Time (DVD) directors: Jean-Pierre Cottet, Guillaume Cottet, 2017

Walter Liedtke, Johannes Vermeer (1632–1675), Department of European Paintings, The Metropolitan Museum of Art October 2003 (
online)
The Lacemaker (c.1669-70), Visual-arts-cork (online).
Jonathan Jones, Vermeer: the artist who taught the world to see ordinary beauty, The Guardian, 8 Feb 2017
ASMR - The Lacemaker by Vermeer, youtube video.
Essentialvermieer.com
Britannica En**cy**clopedia

THE SWING

Philip Conisbee, French Genre Painting in the Eighteenth Century, published by the National Gallery of Art, Center for Advanced Study in the Visual Arts, Distributed by Yale University Press, 2007
Jennifer Dawn Milam ,Playful Constructions and Fragonard's Swinging Scenes, Eighteenth-Century Studies, 33(4): 543-559 June 2000.
Donald Posner The Swinging Women of Watteau and Fragonard, The Art Bulletin Volume 64, 1982 - Issue 1.
Alina Cohen, Undressing the Erotic Symbolism in "The Swing," Fragonard's Decadent Masterpiece, ARTSY, 09 Sept 2019 (online).
Michael D. Walker. Foliage as a Modifier of Erotica and Indicator of Politics in Fragonard Paintings, Virginia Commonwealth University
Margherita Cole, The Scandalous Symbolism Behind Jean-Honoré Fragonard's Masterpiece "The Swing", My Modern Met, on November 15, 2019 (online).
WALLACE COLLECTION official website

PSYCHE REVIVED BY CUPID'S KISS

Giuliano Pisani, Antonio Canova: la freccia di Amore e Psiche, in Atti e Memorie dell'Accademia Galileiana di Scienze, Lettere ed Arti in Padova, CXXX - Parte III, Padova 2018, pp. 297-317, 2019
Isabella Teotochi Albrizzi, Manlio Pastore Stocchi, and Gianni Venturi, Opere Di Scultura e Di Plastica Di Antonio Canova. (Bassano del Grappa: Istituto di Nicerca per gli Studi su Canova e il Neoclassicismo, 2003), 76.
Marina mattei, The tale of Cupid and Psyche : myth in art from antiquity to Canova, Pub-

lished 2012

Arte Opere e Artisti, https://www.arteopereartisti.it/amore-e-psiche/

Istituto Italiano Edizioni Atlas, Amore e psiche https://www.youtube.com/watch?v=-5DO4cht_tN0

M. G. Bernardini Favola di Amore e Psiche. Il mito nell'arte dall'antichità a Canova. Ediz. Illustrata, L'Erma di Bretschneider, 2012

Honour, Hugh. "Canova's Studio Practice-I: The Early Years." The Burlington Magazine 114, no. 828 (1972): 146-59. Accessed May 21, 2021. http://www.jstor.org/stable/876904.

Gilroy-Ware, Cora. (2017). Antonio Canova and the Whatever Body. Open Library of Humanities. 3. 10.16995/olh.67.

Musee Louvre, http://musee.louvre.fr/oal/psyche/psyche_acc_en.html

Jonathan Jones. How I finally warmed to Antonio Canova, rival to Michelangelo, The Guardian, 24 Aug 2010 (online)

Idalis Love, The Genius of Antonio Canova: A Neoclassic Marvel, The collectoor.com April 15, 2021 (online)

The North American Review 29, no. 65 (1829): 441-78. http://www.jstor.org/stable/25102807.

FOTO: Creative Commons Attribution-Share Alike 2.0 Generic license.

THE THIRD OF MAY 1808

Mahnaz Bassir, To what extent does the third of may 1808 involve idealization?, York University 2017

Anne Leader, Goya Paints Third of May 1808: Execution of the Citizens of Madrid, In Great Events from History: The 19th Century, 1801-1900. 4 vols. Ed. John Powell, 203-5. Pasadena: Salem Press.

Xavier de Salas, Goya, Published by Mayflower Books, 1978

Robert Hughes, Goya, Knopf Books, 2003.

Sarah Carr-Gomm, Francisco Goya, Grange Books, 2006

Hagen, Rose-Marie and Hagen, Rainer. Francisco Goya, 1746–1828. Köln: Taschen, 2007. pp. 28–29.

The unflinching eye, The Guardian online article, 2003

Siri Hustvedt, Look out - he's behind you, The Observer Art, The Guardian online article Sun 19 Oct 2003

Manuela B. Mena Marqués, 3 de mayo de 1808 en Madrid: los fusilamientos de patriotas madrileños, El [Goya], Museo Do Prado website.

Goya par Laurent Matheron, Schulz e Truille, Parsi, 1858

THE GRANDE ODALISQUE

Van Liere, Eldon N. "Ingres' 'Raphael and the Fornarina': Reverence and Testimony." Arts Magazine. 52 (1981): 108-15.
Riopelle, Christopher. "Ingres and Sensuality and Refinement." The Art Quarterly of the National Art Collections Fund (1998): 50-54.
Ternois, Daniel. "L'Éros ingresque." Revue de L'art 64 (1984): 35-56.
Fatema Mernissi, L'harem e l'Occidente, Giunti, 2000.
Jean-Yves Maigne, Gilles Chatellier and Hélène Norlöff, Extra vertebrae in Ingres' La Grande Odalisque JR SOC MED, 2004.
Study for La Grande Odalisque, The Courtauld, https://courtauld.ac.uk/highlights/study-for-la-grande-odalisque/
Maigne, Jean-Yves, Gilles Chatellier and Hélène Norlöff. "Extra Vertebrae in Ingres' La Grande Odalisque." Journal of the Royal Society of Medicine. 97.7 (2004): 342-44.
Danya Epstein, Pathology and Imagination: Ingres's Anatomical Distortions, 2015
Flam, Jack. "Ingres and Matisse." Apollo 484 (October 2000): 20-25.
Betzer, Sarah. "Ingres's Shadows." The Art Bulletin 95.1 (2013): 78-101.
Between Neoclassicism and Romanticism: Ingres, La Grande Odalisque Essay by Dr. Bryan Zygmont, Khan Academy
Kimmelman, Michael. "Ingres at the Louvre: His Pursuit of Higher Reality." New York Times. March 24, 2006, http://www.nytimes.com/2006/03/24/arts/design/24ingr.html?pagewanted=all
Feaver, William. "Why all Ingres is Erotic." ArtNews, 1 September 2006. http://www.artnews.com/2006/09/01/why-all-ingres-is-erotic/
Steven Zucker and Beth Harris, Painting colonial culture: Ingres's La Grand Odalisque, Khan Academy (online)

WANDERER ABOVE THE SEA FOG

Haladyn, Julian Jason. "Friedrich's 'Wanderer': Paradox of the Modern Subject." RACAR: Revue D'art Canadienne / Canadian Art Review, vol. 41, no. 1, 2016, pp. 47–61.
MIGUELANGEL GAETE, From Caspar David Friedrich's Wanderer above the Sea of Fog to the iCloud: A Comparative Analysis between theRomantic Concept of the Sublime and Cyberspace, 2020, Journal of Comparative Literature and Aesthetics
Christopher P Jones, How to Read Paintings: Wanderer above the Sea of Fog by Caspar David Friedrich, Mar 3, 2020, MEDIUM (online).
Raffaella Arpiani, Il viandante sul mare di nebbia, Arte essenziale (youtube video)
Exhibition Catalogue: Caspar David Friedrich. Die Underling der Romantic in Essen ind

Hamburg, Firmer Verlag, München (December 2006), page 267.
Idrobo, Carlos (November 2012). "He Who Is Leaving ... The Figure of the Wanderer in Nietzsche's Also sprach Zarathustra and Caspar David Friedrich's Der Wanderer über dem Nebelmeer". Nietzsche-Studien. 41 (1): 78–103. doi:10.1515/niet.2012.41.1.78. S2CID 155017448. (Online) (Print).
"Wanderer above the Sea of Fog", Artble (online)
Dan Scott, A Closer Look at Wanderer Above the Sea of Fog by Caspar David Friedrich February 10, 2020, DRAWPAINTACADEMY (online)

LIBERT LEADING THE PEOPLE

Dr. Bryan Zygmont, "Eugène Delacroix, Liberty Leading the People," in Smarthistory, November 22, 2015
Yashoda Chaulaga, Visual Position and Juxtaposition: An Analytical Study of Liberty Leading the People and Moon-Woman Cuts the Circle December 2018 Tribhuvan University Journal 32(2):191-202
Collins, Neil (ed.). Romanticism in Art. Visual-arts-Cork.com, 2016.
Agulhon, M. "Marianne into Battle: Republican Imagery and Symbolism in France, 1789–1880," Cambridge, U.K. Cambridge University Press, 1981. pp. 38–42
Gaudibert, P. "Delacroix et le romantisme re´volutionnaire," Europe 41, no. 408 (1963): 4–21.
Hadjinicolaou, N. "La Liberte´ guidant le peuple de Delacroix devant son premier public," Actes de la recherche en sciences sociales (1979): 3–26.
Hamilton, G. H. "The iconographical origins of Delacroix's Liberty Leading the People," in Studies in Art and Literature for Bella da Costa Greene. Edited by Dorothy Eugenia Miner. Princeton, N. J.: Princeton University Press, 1954. 55–66.Jobert Delacroix, B. Princeton, N. J.: Princeton University Press, 1998. 128–33.
Yvonne Korshak, "The Liberty Cap as a Revolutionary Symbol in America and France," Smithsonian Studies in American Art (Autumn 1987), pp. 52-69
Encyclopedia Britannica

THE GREAT WAVE OF KANAGAWA

Julyan Cartwright and Hisami Nakamura, What kind of a wave is Hokusai's Great wave off Kanagawa? May 2009, Notes and Records of The Royal Society 63(2):119-135.
On Hokusai's Great Wave Off Kanagawa: Localization, Linearity And A Rogue Wave in

Sub-Antarctic Waters J. M. Dudley, V. Sarano And F. Dias, Notes Rec. R. Soc. (2013) 67, 159–164.

Science and Culture: Dissecting the Great Wave, Stephen Ornes, PNAS September 16, 2014 111 (37) 13245.

The Local and the Global: Hokusai's Great Wave in Contemporary Product Design, Christine M. E. Guth, 2012 Massachusetts Institute of Technology, DesignIssues: Volume 28, Number 2

Kuan, Christine. "Hokusai: A World of Genius." Artsy, 22 Sept. 2013, www.artsy.net/article/christine-hokusai-a-world-of-genius

The Conversation, Friday essay: from the Great Wave to Starry Night, how a blue pigment changed the world, Hugh Davies, 20 Luglio 2017 (online)

John-Paul Stonard, Hokusai: the Great Wave that swept the world, The Gurdian, Fri 19 May 2017 (online)

Dan Tham and Junko Ogura Why the 'Great Wave' has mystified art lovers for generations, CNN, updated, Updated 18th March 2019 (online)

A Brief History Of 'The Great Wave': Japan's Most Famous Artwork, Culture Trip, 6 June 2017 (online)

THE NINTH WAVE

"The Ninth Wave". Hermitage Museum. Archived from the original on 4 November 2013. Retrieved 1 November 2013.

"Aivazovsky, I. K. The Ninth Wave. 1850". Auburn University. Retrieved 10 December 2013. '

Elina Sopo, 'Ivan Konstantinovich Aivazovsky', in Art & Athmosphere, Helsinki: Finnish National Gallery (2013) 2013, Art & Athmosphere

Detail from "The Ninth Wave" "The Ninth Wave," painted in 1850, is Aivazovsky's most famous work and is an archetypal image for the artist.

La Nona Onda, Finestre sull'arte (online), 2018

Thoughts, Reviews & Translations by Dmitry Fadeyev, The ninth wave 2013 https://fadeyev.net/the-ninth-wave/

Amidst the waves. 20 fascinating facts about Ivan Aivazovsky, the artist most loved by the Russians, Arthive (online)

Paintings of the World, Ivan Aivazovsky, The Art Gallery, Youtube video

THE GLEANERS

Fratello, Bradley (December 2003). "France embraces Millet: the intertwined fates of The Gleaners and The Angelus". The Art Bulletin. The Art Bulletin, Vol. 85, No. 4. 85 (4): 685–701.
Jean-François Millet's Painting Composition Analysis, The Gleaners and the Golden Angles, Lin Kuang, Kelsey Brow, Molly Huang
Lin Kuang, Analysis on the Evolution of Millet's Artworks of The Gleaners, Bulletin of National Museum of History, 2011.
"Story behind the picture – The Gleaners". University of St. Andrews.
Herbert, Robert. "City vs. Country: The Rural Image in French Painting from Millet to Gauguin." ArtForum 8, no. 6 (Feb. 1970): 44–55
Fratello, Bradley (Dec. 2003). «France embraces Millet: the intertwined fates of Des Glaneuses and The Angelus». The Art Bulletin. 85 (4). The Art Bulletin, Vol. 85, No. 4. pp. 685–701. J
Kimmelman, Michael (August 27, 1999). "Art Review: Plucking Warmth From Millet's Light". The New York Times. New York City.
"Millet's The Gleaners". Smarthistory at Khan Academy. Retrieved February 27, 2013.

LUNCHEON ON THE GRASS

Chapman, Ian. "Luncheon on the Grass with Manet and Bow Wow Wow: Still Disturbing After All These Years." Music in Art, vol. 35, no. 1/2, 2010, pp. 95–104. JSTOR, www.jstor.org/stable/41818609. Accessed 21 May 2021.
Andersen, W. V. (2005). Manet: The picnic & the prostitute. Boston: Editions Fabriart
Bourdieu, P. (2014). Manet: A symbolic revolution. Novos Estudos CEBRAP, (99), 121-135.
Juzefovič, Agnieška. (2016). Creative transformations in visual arts of early french modernism: treatment of nude body. CREATIVITY STUDIES. 9. 10.3846/23450479.2015.1112854.
Siyu, Gao. The lunch on the grass, Carleton University April 2017
Læssøe, R. (2005). Édouard Manet's "Le Déjeuner sur l'herbe" as a Veiled Allegory of Painting. Artibus et Historiae, 26, 195-220.
Melanie Desliens Flint, "The Luncheon on the Grass" was outrageous, here is why... MEDIUM (online) Nov 15, 2016
Dr. Beth Harris and Dr. Steven Zucker, "Édouard Manet, Le déjeuner sur l'herbe (Luncheon on the Grass)," in Smarthistory (online video), November 21, 2015.

WHISTLER'S MOTHER

James C Harris, Arrangement in Grey and Black, No. 1: Portrait of the Painter's Mother, January 2006 Archives of General Psychiatry 62(12):1294-5

Peter Schjeldahl, Whistler's Mother: Portrait of an Extraordinary Life, THE NEW YORKER, 2015.

J. M. Whistler, The Gentle Art of Making Enemies, 1890

Daniel E. Sutherland and Georgia Toutziari Whistler's Mother: Portrait of an Extraordinary Life, Yale University Press, 2018

Kathleen Pyne, Ch. 3 - James McNeill Whistler and the Religion of Art, from ART AND THE HIGHER LIFE: PAINTING AND EVOLUTIONARY THOUGHT IN LATE NINETEENTH-CENTURY AMERICA, 1996

Caitlin Doley, Age and Aesthetics in James Abbott McNeill Whistler's 'Arrangement in Grey and Black: Portrait of the Painter's Mother' (1871)

'The Red Rag,' Published in Whistler, James McNeill, "The Red Rag"in 'Celebrities at Home. No. XCII. Mr Whistler at Cheyne-Walk,' The World, 22 May 1878, pp. 4-5 [GM, A.2]. Reproduced in Whistler, James McNeill, The Gentle Art of Making Enemies, 2nd ed., London and New York, 1892, pp. 126-8.

Ted Snell, Here's looking at: 'Whistler's Mother, THE CONVERSATION, 2016 (online)

Kathryn Hughes Whistler's Mother review – a painting that's not what it seems, The Guardian, 2018 (online)

BAL DU MOULIN DE LA GALETTE

Georges Rivière, Renoir et Ses Amis, 1921, H. Floury Editeur.

Gilles Néret, "Renoir. Painter of Happiness", Hardcover, 2009

Harris, Sue, and Queen Mary. "Renoir's Paris: The City as Film Set." South Central Review, vol. 28, no. 3, 2011, pp. 84–102. JSTOR, www.jstor.org/stable/41261503.

The Mixing of Classes in Renoir's Bal au Moulin de la Galette

Come Una Fotografia. Ballando Con Renoir, Al Moulin De La Galette, Francesca Grego, arte.it, 2020

The Story Behind Renoir's 'Bal du moulin de la Galette', MY MODERN MET, By Kelly Richman-Abdou, 2020

Caudio Strinati, Dialogues "Raccontare l'arte", L'opera del lunedì - Renoir "Bal au moulin de la Galette", youtube video 2021

Canvasing the Masterpieces, Bal du moulin della Gallette by Renoir, KAZOART, Laurel Bouye, 2019

Renoir, Moulin de la Galette, Khan Academy, video

Dance at Le Moulin de la Galette (1876), Visual Art Cork

A SUNDAY AFTERNOON ON THE ISLAND OF LA GRANDE-JATTE

Inge Fiedler. "A Technical Evaluation of the Grande Jatte." Art Institute of Chicago Museum Studies, vol. 14, no. 2, 1989, pp. 173–245. JSTOR, www.jstor.org/stable/4108750
Flux, Paul. Georges Seurat (Life and Work Of...). Heinemann Educational Books, 2002
John House, Reading the Grande Jatte, Art Institute of Chicago Museum Studies Vol. 14, No. 2, The Grande Jatte at 100 (1989), pp. 114-131+240-241 (20 pages).
Benin, Nikola. A Sunday Afternoon on the Island of La Grande Jatte (Un dimanche après-midi à l'Île de la Grande Jatte) by Georges Seurat. 10.13140/RG.2.2.19749.24802, (2020).
Andrey V., A Sunday Afternoon on the Island of La Grande Jatte - A Study, Widewalls (online), January 28, 2018
BBC Documentary, The Private Life of a Masterpiece (2005) Series 4, Georges Seurat: A Sunday Afternoon on the Island of La Grande Jatte.
Jeffrey Meyers, Essay: The Meaning of La Grande Jatte , The London Magazine (online), Apr 14, 2020
A Sunday Afternoon on the Island of La Grande Jatte, ARTBLE (online)
   Seurat, Georges. "A Sunday on La Grande Jatte — 1884". The Art Institute of Chicago. Artic Edu (online) Retrieved 17 May 2021.

CAFE' TERACE AT NIGHT

Van Gogh's Last Supper: A Nonfiction Book Proposal, Jared Baxter
Aurier, Albert: Les Isolés: Vincent van Gogh , Mercure de France, January, 1890.
Stein, Susan Alyson, Editor: Van Gogh: A Retrospective , Macmillan Pub. Co., 1986.Stolwijk, Chris and Veenenbos, Han: Account Book of Theo van Gogh, Primavera Pers, 2004
Interesting Art Stories: 24. Café Terrace at Night, Vincent van Gogh, ACJ Art Academy (Youtube video)
Jansen, Leo and Luijten, Hans and Bakker, Nienke, Editors: Vincent van Gogh – The Letters: TheComplete Illustrated and Annotated Edition, (Vol. 1-6), Thames & Hudson, 2009.
Jared Baxter, Van Gogh's Last Supper: Transforming "the guise of observable reality," January, 2014
Art History Supplement, Vol. 4, No. 1.
Jared Baxter Van Gogh's Last Supper: Transforming "the guise of observable reality," July, 2014, The Anistoriton Journal of History, Archaeology and Art History, Vol. 14, No. 1.

Café Terrace at Night, 1888 by Vincent Van Gogh, www.vincentvangogh.org/cafe-at-night.jsp

Why Vincent's Cafe Terrace At Night Is A Symbolist Last Supper: PART 1 OF 2 MARCH 9, 2016, think.iafor.org

THE LADY OF SHALOTT

Allyson McMahon Bourke, Tennyson ennyson's Lady of Shalott in Pr s Lady of Shalott in Pre-Raphaelite Ar e-Raphaelite Art: Exonerated Artist or Fallen Woman, College of William & Mary - Arts & Sciences, 1996

Loreena Mckennitt, Testi e Traduzioni, (online)

John William Waterhouse, The Lady of Shalott, 1888, oil on canvas, Tate Gallery, London.

Simonetta Falchi, The Lady of Shalott in Pre-Raphaelite Painting

Elizabeth Nelson. "Pictorial Interpretations of "The Lady of Shalott": The Lady in her Boat." Adapted from the author's "Tennyson and the Ladies of Shalott, Ladies of Shalott: A Victorian Masterpiece and its Contexts",(Opens in a new window) Victorian Web(1979)

THE STARRY NIGHT

Vecchio Testamento

Whitney, Charles A. (September 1986). "The Skies of Vincent van Gogh". Art History. 9 (3): 351–362

Bradford A. Richardson, MD, Alexandra M. Rusyniak, W. George Rusyniak, Jr, MD, Charles B. Rodning, MD, PhD, Neuroanatomical Interpretation of the Painting Starry Night by Vincent van Gogh, Neurosurgery, Volume 81, Issue 3, September 2017, Pages 389–396

Ghani, Dahlan. (2014). The Scream & Starry Night: Emotions, symbol & motives. 20. 331-339. 10.5209/rev-ESMP.2014.v20.n1.45235

L'opera del lunedì, la notte stellata di Vincent Van Gogh, Dialogues, raccontare l'Arte)youtube video)

Soth, Lauren. "Van Gogh's Agony." Art Bulletin 68, no. 2 (1986): 301-313

Boime, Albert (December 1984). "Van Gogh's Starry Night: A History of Matter and a Matter of History". Arts Magazine. 59 (4): 86–103

Jirat-Wasiutynski, Vojtech (December 1993). "Vincent van Gogh's Paintings of Olive Trees and Cypresses from St.-Remy". Art Bulletin. 75 (4)

Layman, Lewis M. "Echoes of Walt Whitman's 'Bare-Bosom'D Night' in Vincent van Gogh's Starry Night." American Notes & Queries 22, no. 7-8 (1984): 105-109

Vincent S. Stassi, Vincent van Gogh's Starry Night: Insights from Poetry, Art History, and Astronomy
Starry Night Analysis, ARTBLE, https://www.artble.com/artists/vincent_van_gogh/paintings/starry_night/more_information/analysis
10 ecrets of Starry Night by Vincent van Gogh, ART ENIGMA, Youtube video, 9 April 2020

THE SCREAM

Wood, Mara-Helen (ed.) (1992). Edvard Munch: The Frieze of Life. Harvard, MA: Yale University Press.
Carroll, Karen Lee. "Artistic Beginnings: The Work of Young Edvard Munch." Studies in Art Education, vol. 36, no. 1, 1994, pp. 7–17. JSTOR, www.jstor.org/stable/1320344.
Fred Prata, Alan Robock and Richard Hamblyn. The Sky in Edvard Munch's The Scream, BAMS 2018
Gary E. Friedlaender, MDcorresponding author and Linda K. Friedlaender, Edvard Munch and The Scream: A Cry for Help, Clin Orthop Relat Res. 2018 Feb; 476(2): 200–202.
Prideaux, Sue. Edvard Munch. Behind the Scream. Harvard, MA: Yale University Press 2005.
Jones, Jonathan (2012). 'Edvard Munch's The Scream Analysed – Interactive'. Retrieved 20 March 2015 from http://www.theguardian.com/artanddesign/interactive/2012/may/03/edvard-munch-scream-interactive
Unn Plahter and Leif Einar Plahter, Munch's paintings: scientific research both recent and in retrospect, 2015
Eggum, A. (1978) 'The theme of death', in Edvard MunchSymbols and Images, 143–53. Washington DC: NationalGallery of Art.
Lentz, Merryl (2014). 'Analysis of The Scream by Edvard Munch'. Retrieved 20 March 2015 from http://www.finearts360.com/index.php/analysis-of-the-scream-by-edvard-munch-7398
Afshin Akhtar-Khavari Fear and Ecological (in)Justice in Edvard Munch's The Scream of Nature
Lanre Bakare, 'Painted by a madman': The Scream graffiti may reveal Munch's state of mind, The Guardian, 22 Feb 2021 (online)

FLAMING JUNE

Alastair Sooke, The erotic masterpiece we nearly lost, 16th November 2016, BBC Culture (online)
Skye Sherwin, Frederic Leighton's Flaming June: the Mona Lisa of the southern hemisphere, The Gurdian, 16 Dicembre 2016 (online)
Rachel Campbell-Johnston, Flaming June will brighten the darkness, The Times, 28 Ottobre 2016 (online)
The Deathly Sleep of Frederic Leighton's Painted Women, Women: A Cultural Review Volume 23, 2012 - Issue 2.
James Gardner, A Sleeper Awakened With Color, , WSJ, June 26, 2015 (online)
Vera Mantengoli, Flaming June, vergine o dark lady? Torna la "ragazza di fuoco", La Repubblica 30 Giugno 2015 (online)
John Haber, Sexuality and Symbolism, Harberarts.com
Meir H. Kryger and MD Isabella Siegel, Sleep in enchanted colors, Cover Art, Sleep Health Volume 3, Issue 4, August 2017, Pages 223-224
Meir H. Kryger, MD Isabella Siegel
Study For Lord Leighton's Flaming June Re-emerges After 120 Years, Artlyst, 2 May 2015

THE SLEEPING GYPSY

Dobyns, Stephen. On the Famous Painting by Rousseau.New England Review and Bread Loaf Quarterly; Middlebury, Vt. Vol. 8, Iss. 4, (Summer 1986): 482
Douglas Cooper, Henri Rousseau: Artiste-Peintre The Burlington Magazine for Connoisseurs, Vol. 85, No. 496 (Jul., 1944), pp. 158+160-165 (7 pages), Published By: Burlington Magazine Publications Ltd
Bush, Elizabeth. Review of The Sleeping Gypsy, by Mordicai Gerstein. Bulletin of the Center for Children's Books, vol. 70 no. 3, 2016, p. 125-126. Project MUSE, doi:10.1353/bcc.2016.0878.
Spencer's painting of the week, Youtube video https://www.youtube.com/watch?v=H_H7yeULk5I
Lam Thi My Da, poesia "On Henri Rousseau's The Sleeping Gypsy"
Henri Rousseau – The Sleeping Gypsy (1897), Artschaft, 2018 (Online)
ENCYCLOPEDIA BRITANNICA,
The Sleeping Gypsy (1897) by Henri Rousseau, Interpretation of Outsider Art (Naif Painting), Visual Art Cork (online).

WHERE DO WE COME FROM? WHAT ARE WE? WHERE ARE WE GOING?

George P. Nicholas, "Where do we come from? What are we? Where are we going?": Gauguin's Questions, Anthropology's Challenges -, Department of Archaeology, Simon Fraser University Burnaby, British Columbia, 2000
Dorra, Henri. The Symbolism of Paul Gauguin : Erotica, Exotica, and the Great Dilemmas of Humanity . Berkeley: University of California Press, 2007
George T. M. Shackelford. Paul Gauguin: Where Do We Come From? What are We? Where are We Going? Museum of Fine Arts, Boston, MFA publications, Museum of Fine Arts, 2013
Harris JC. Where do we come from? What are we? Where are we going? Arch Gen Psychiatry. 2011 Nov;68(11):1090. doi: 10.1001/archgenpsychiatry.2011.143. PMID: 22065526
Humphrey, Nicholas. (2007). The society of selves. Philosophical transactions of the Royal Society of London. Series B, Biological sciences. 362. 745-54. 10.1098/rstb.2006.2007
Anastasia V. Klykova, Iconographic Research of Paul Gauguin's Masterpiece «Caricature of Tahiti Governor Lacascade, Siberian Federal University 2009
Dr. Noelle Paulson, "A-Level: Paul Gauguin, Where do we come from? What are we? Where are we going?," in Smarthistory, July 25, 2017, https://smarthistory.org/gauguin-where-do-we-come-from-what-are-we-where-are-we-going-2/
Where Do We Come From? What Are We? Where Are We Going? by Paul Gauguin, Joy of Museums (online)
Raffaella Arpiani. Gauguin: Da dove veniamo? Chi siamo? Dove andiamo, Arte Essenziale, Youtube video

THE ARTIST'S GARDEN AT GIVERNY

Kopinski, Eric & Burley, Jon. (2013). Giverny: Claude Monnet's Garden Retreat. 35. 38-41
Kirk Varnedoe, MONET AND HIS GARDENS, April 2, 1978, New York Times archives https://www.nytimes.com/1978/04/02/archives/monet-and-his-gardens.html
Steves, R. (n.d.). Giverny and Monet's Garden. Retrieved from Rick Steves' Europe: http://www.ricksteves.com/plan/destinations/france/giverny.htm
Lisa R. Brody et al., "To Varnish or Not to Varnish?," Yale University Art Gallery Bulletin (2010): 122–23, 125, fig. 1.
Wildenstein, Daniel, Claude Monet : catalogue raisonné Claude Monet. 1, 1840-1881, peintures, Bibliothèque des Arts ,Wildenstein institute, Paris, 1974
Ann Dumas, Painting the Modern Garden: Monet to Matisse, exh. cat. (London: Cleveland Museum of Art, 2015), 212, 221, no. 95
"Claude Monet - Le jardin de l'artiste à Giverny". Musée d'Orsay - Collections. Musée

d'Orsay. Retrieved 18 April 2016

Fabienne Boursier. La représentation du jardin dans l'œuvre de Gustave Caillebotte : une peinture documentaire, entre illustration et art. Art et histoire de l'art. 2014

Daily Art magazine, https://www.dailyartmagazine.com/claude-monets-garden-giverny/

Claude Monet Gallery, The Artist's Garden at Giverny, https://www.cmonetgallery.com/artists-garden-at-giverny.aspx

Hammond, Jeff. "How Japan's Art Inspired the West." The Japan Times, 14 Aug. 2014, www.japantimes.co.jp/culture/2014/08/14/arts/how-japans-art-inspired-the-west/#.W-IkznpKi3U

LES DEMOISELLES D'AVIGNON

Suzanne Preston Blier. 2019. Picasso's Demoiselles. The Untold Origins of a Modern Masterpiece. Durham: Duke University

Andersen Wayne . Picasso's Brothel Les Demoiselles d'Avignon. New York, New York Other Press , 2002.

Shulamit Almog. Les demoiselles d'avignon: painting prostitution, delineating law Cardozo Arts & Ent. LJ 36 (2018): 63.

David lomas, in another frame: les demoiselles d'avignon and physical anthropology, in picasso's les demoiselles d'avignon 104 (christopher green, ed., 2001)

Leo Steinberg, The Philosophical Brothel, 44 OCTOBER 7, 43 (1988).

The Complexity of Creativity: Les Demoiselles D'Avignon as a Cognitive-Historical Laboratory

Subrata Dasgupta Pages 377-394 | Published online: 19 Oct 2019

Khan Academy, Arts Blog, Analisi dell'opera

THE KISS

Audiey Kao. Virtual Mentor, ART OF MEDICINE, Gustav Klimt's The Kiss, American Medical Association Journal of Ethics, February 2000, Volume 2, Number 2: 13-14

Julio Vives Chillida, "El significado iconográfico de El beso (los enamorados), de Gustav Klimt", comunicación al primer Coup de Fouet Art nouveau International Congress, Barcelona, junio de 2013

Svitlana Shiells, Japanese Aesthetics and Gustav Klimt: In Pursuit of a New Voice, 2018

Dwyer, Chris. "Gustav Klimt and his enduring 'Kiss'", CNN Style, February 27, 2018

Jonathan Jones, The Last Romantic, The Guardian, 22 Sept. 2001

Gustav Klimt - Il bacio, ARS EUROPA, (youtube video)
Christopher P Jones, How to Read Paintings: The Kiss by Gustav Klimt, A sumptuous celebration of love that may also suggest impending tragedy, Jun 7-2020, mediuim.com (online)
Jonathan Jones, Tammam Azzam's Kiss: an unromantic commentary on the Syrian conflict
Chris Gaylord, Gustav Klimt: Why some say 'The Kiss' is better than the 'Mona Lisa', CS Monitor (online) July 14, 2012

THE ENIGMA OF THE HOUR

G. de Chirico, Statues, meubles et généraux, «Bulletin de l'Effort Moderne», 38, ottobre 1927, pp. 3-6; ora in Giorgio de Chirico, Scritti/1 cit., p. 827
GIORGIO DE CHIRICO. CATALOGO GENERALE OPERE DAL 1913-1975. VOL 4/2018 A CURA DELLA FONDAZIONE GIORGIO E ISA DE CHIRICO
G. De Chirico, Sull'Arte metafisica, 1919
Francesco Santoro, Tempo e spazio Nell'opera Metafisica di Giorgio De Chirico
ADRIANO ALTAMIRA: DE CHIRICO E DUCHAMP
RICCARDO DOTTORI: THE METAPHYSICAL PARABLE IN GIORGIO DE CHIRICO'S PAINTING, METAFISICA 2006 | N° 5-6
Baldacci, Paolo (1 May 2017). "Giorgio de Chirico, The Enigma of the Hour (1910): The First Conceptual Work of Art", The Brooklyn Rail. Retrieved 1 July 2020
G. de Chirico - Casella, «Rassegna musicale», 1943
G. de Chirico, Discorso sul meccanismo del pensiero, in «Documento», Roma, maggio 1943; ora in ivi pp.534-539
Riccardo Dottori. Giorgio de Chirico. Immagini metafisiche. Milano, La nave di Teseo, 2018

THE PERSISTENCE OF MEMORY

Michael Salcman, Towson University, The Persistence of Memory (1931) by Salvador Dalí (1904-1989), PubMed
Staff editor (28 January 1989). "Dali, The Flamboyant Surrealist". The Vindicator. The death of Salvador Dali evokes the image of his most famous painting, Persistence of Memory, (online).
Dali, The Persistence of Memory, Khan Acedemy and Smarthistory, (youtube video)
The Persistence of Memory, Salvador Dalì | Painting Analysis, Sigfrido Millequadri, (youtube video)
Dalì e la Persistenza della memoria, Raffaella Arpiani - Arte essenziale, (youtube video)

"Dali's The Persistence of Memory". Smarthistory and Khan Academy, (online)
"Salvador Dalí. The Persistence of Memory. 1931". MoMa, (online)
Britannica Encyclopedia

GUERNICA

Antony Beevor "La guerra civile spagnola", New York Times (articolo del 27 Aprile 1937), Pablo Picasso paintings, Quotes, & Biography – WIKIPEDIA
Clark TJ, Picasso and Truth: From Cubism to Guernica. Princeton, NJ: Princeton University Press, 2013
Rachel Wischnitzer, Picasso's "Guernica". A Matter of Metaphor, Artibus et Historiae Vol. 6, No. 12 (1985), pp. 153-172 (20 pages)
Chipp, H. B. 1988. Picasso's Guernica: History, transformation, meaning. Berkeley: University of California Press.
Martin, R. 2003. Picasso's war: The destruction of Guernica, and the masterpiece that changed the world. New York: Plume
Beverly Ray, Analyzing Political Art to Get at Historical Fact: Guernica and the Spanish Civil War, The Social Studies ·January 2006
Lynn Robinson, "Picasso, Guernica", Khan Academy, (online)
Richard Rhodes, "Guernica: Horror and inspiration", Bulletin of the Atomic Scientists 69(6) 19–25
George Steer, "The Tragedy of Guernica", The Times, 27 April 1937
Vidal C (1997) La Destruction de Guernica, trans. Peter Miller. Chapter 9, Guernica, demolished. Available at: http://www.buber.net/Basque/History/guernica-ix.html
Simbologia di GUERNICA - Pablo Picasso - I SIMBOLI NELL'ARTE – ARS Europe (youtube video)
Raffaella Arpiani, Picasso e Guernica, Arte Essenziale, (youtube video)
Picasso's Guernica, Great Art Explained, (Youtube video)

Printed in Great Britain
by Amazon